Endorsements

of *How To Cut America's Divorce Rate in Half* by Mike McManus

How to Cut America's Divorce Rate in Half is a timely and important work. As we look to secure a better future for our children there is nothing more fundamental than the strengthening of the American family. The first step in strengthening the family is reforming no-fault divorce. Mike McManus' latest work provides a strategy to reform this broken system.
Tony Perkins, President, Family Research Council and author of the nation's first covenant marriage law.

Divorce is the most serious force for family destruction in the Western world today, and therefore it is also the greatest threat to both civic order and freedom itself. Mike McManus's proposal for mutual consent divorce and other reforms offers the realistic prospect of drastically reducing divorce rate by half and of creating a needed national dialogue on this unaddressed crisis.
Stephen Baskerville, Ph.D., Associate Professor of Government at Patrick Henry College and author of "Taken Into Custody: The War Against Fathers, Marriage, and the Family"

As a divorce lawyer, I see every day how much carnage and anger the divorce process causes, and how damaging it is to men, women and children alike. But there is an immense gap between the dissatisfaction that comes out of the process, and actually doing something constructive about it. People need to realize that the real cause of their problems is not their parents, their ex, the other sex in general, or the lawyers or the judges. They need to raise their horizons and see that the real problem is divorce itself. Just as difficult, is identifying specific social actions, public policies and laws that can help to reduce divorce. This book bridges those gaps, from dissatisfaction to understanding, to clear policy ideas, to sensible, proven techniques to organize for effective advocacy. Mike McManus has a track record of "being the change" that he advocates, with his decades of work building Community Marriage Policies and many other efforts to protect marriage. With this book, he points the way towards changes that could reduce divorce by 50%, as part of a cultural revolution just as profound and dramatic as the one that gave us our present-day levels of divorce, cohabitation and single parenthood.

John Crouch, Director, Americans For Divorce Reform

The divorce reform proposed by Mike McManus is revolutionary and absolutely unprecedented. It would save millions of marriages and stabilize American families, giving kids a much better start in life. I can't think of any reform that could make America a better place."

Don Wildmon, Chairman, American Family Association.

Every pastor is stunned by the number of couples in his church who divorce. Few of them realize that in four out of five cases, one spouse does NOT want the divorce, but is forced to accept it because the law actually grants every divorce, shattering the lives of children. Mike McManus puts his finger on a simple but profound answer: require that in cases involving children that both parents would have to agree to a divorce, except in cases of adultery or physical abuse. I believe this change in the law could cut the divorce rate in half. That would spare 500,000 children from seeing their parents divorce each year, and save $50-$100 billion in taxpayer funds. This is an issue that should be taken to those running for state or federal offices in this election year.

Rev. Richard Cizik, Vice President of the National Association of Evangelicals

The American people have always leaned to the view that divorce laws are not strict enough, particularly as they relate to the raising of children. Michael McManus' proposed mutual consent law is certain to appeal to a large segment of the populous.

George Gallup, Jr. Founder George H. Gallup International Institute

Michael McManus is to be commended for sounding the alarm on the devastatingly negative impact No Fault Divorce has had on our society. However, perhaps the most valuable thing about *How to Cut the Divorce Rate in Half* is that McManus does not just curse the darkness—he lights candles in that darkness. He draws a blueprint for how we can substantially remedy the catastrophe of divorce in our nation and how ordinary citizens can make a difference. This is a much-needed and encouraging book.

Dr. Richard Land, President. The Southern Baptist Convention's Ethics & Religious Liberty Commission

The Catholic Church does not believe in divorce at all, but is encouraged that polls reveal that by a 2-1 margin Americans believe it should "be harder than it is now for married couples with young children to get a civil divorce (61% to 35%)." *How To Cut America's Divorce Rate in Half* suggests how to do that, by requiring written mutual consent of both a mother and father before any divorce is granted. By giving the spouse who wants to save the marriage an equal voice with an unhappy mate, many marriages could be restored, perhaps saving most of them.

Bishop Gerald A. Gettelfinger, Catholic Diocese of Evansville

We need to reform our divorce laws, as Mike McManus suggests, replacing unilateral (or "no-fault") divorce with mutual consent divorce where children are involved. This reform would, in the words of one prominent divorce attorney, "not only influence the decision to divorce, but the behavior and choices that lead to divorce." McManus recognizes that laws governing marriage and divorce decisively shape people's understanding of the meaning of marriage and affect their behavior and choices. Laws are not neutral. They have an impact—for better or worse—on the marriage culture. Getting the right laws into place is among the most critical tasks we face.

Robert P. George, McCormick Professor of Jurisprudence, Princeton University

The book Mike McManus has written makes a valuable contribution at this point in our history, on the eve of the election of a new president. He restores the critical focus on divorce law reform that was overtaken and overshadowed by the struggle over same-sex marriage.
Katherine Spaht, Professor Emeritus, Landry Professor of Law, Louisiana State University

With precise reasoning, overwhelming data, and a passionate heart, Mike McManus creates a marriage manifesto. A compelling piece, that when implemented, will systemically and significantly raise the quality of life for all Americans for generations. The evidence is clear and it is time to act. Mike McManus makes a case for churches, social entities and government – both State and National – to act. The more quickly we act the more quickly we will be safer, richer, smarter, stronger, happier and healthier. This is a no-brainer strategy with nothing to lose and everything to gain.
Pastor Jeff Meyers. Christ Lutheran Church, Overland Park, Kansas

In *How to Cut America's Divorce Rate In Half*, Mike McManus gives a call to action we must not ignore! In this short book, Mike lays out the facts and figures in a strategy for helping change the divorce culture. Read it, act and let your voice be heard!
David and Claudia Arp, founders Marriage Alive International and authors of "10 Great Dates Before You Say 'I Do.'"

Michael McManus provides a compelling case for reforming divorce law in America. His policy proposals are right on the money; they would go a long way to renewing the culture of marriage in our nation.
W. Bradford Wilcox, Ph.D., associate professor of sociology at the University of Virginia and member of the James Madison Society, Princeton University

❧

How To Cut America's Divorce Rate In Half

By Mike McManus

With a Foreword by Mike Huckabee, Former Governor of Arkansas

How To Cut America's Divorce Rate In Half
Written by Michael J. McManus
With a Foreword by Mike Huckabee, Former Governor of Arkansas
Composition, cover design, and production by
  Marco Ciavolino (Enktesis, LLC / enktesis.com)

Published by Marriage Savers, Inc.
9311 Harrington Dr.
Potomac, MD 20854
(301) 469-5873
marriagesavers.org

Related Sites:
ReformDivorce.org
ReduceDivorce.org

First Edition

File Information
* Name: MARR080728DivorceBook_v29P.doc
* Save Date/Time: 9/21/2008 9:11 PM

1. Marriage and divorce, 2. Families and children, 3. Divorce law and reform

ISBN: 978-1-60702-688-4

Other books by Michael J. McManus

Marriage Savers: Helping Your Friends and
Family Avoid Divorce

50 Practical Ways To Take Our Kids
Back from the World

Insuring Marriage: 25 Proven Ways
to Prevent Divorce

Living Together: Myths, Risks & Answers
By Mike & Harriet McManus

Mike McManus has written the nationally syndicated column, "Ethics & Religion" since 1981. He is President and Co-Founder with his wife, Harriet, of Marriage Savers, a non-profit organization that has helped the clergy of 223 cities to create Community Marriage Policies that have reduced divorce and cohabitation rates and increased marriage rates. This is his first book to call for a political solution to America's divorce rate, which is the highest in the world.

Dedication

This book is dedicated to Harriet, my wife of nearly 43 years who has been the joy of my life, the co-creator of our Marriage Savers ministry, and mother of three remarkable sons who married wonderful daughters-in-law who have blessed us with six grandchildren.

This book is also dedicated to more than ten thousand pastors and priests who created Community Marriage Policies and Marriage Savers Congregations, many of which have virtually eliminated divorce and to thousands of trained Mentor Couples who are the true "marriage savers."

I am also grateful to Chuck Stetson who inspired and underwrote the launching of this effort to reform No Fault Divorce and to Marco Ciavolino (www.enktesis.com) who created www.marriagesavers.org, www.ReformDivorce.org and designed this book in record time.

☙

How To Cut America's Divorce Rate in Half

Table of Contents

Foreword by Mike Huckabee, Former Governor of Arkansas

Divorce is wreaking havoc on America. One of the single worst decisions of our judicial system has been the creation of No Fault Divorce. When it is easier to get out of a marriage than it is to get out of a car loan, something is terribly wrong. When families are destroyed, often because of the selfish actions of one of the partners, something is wrong. When children are innocent victims and have to grow up in a broken home, something is wrong. Mike McManus gets it right.

The idea to replace the No Fault Divorce with a Mutual Consent Divorce is a great start, but is only part of the solution. The sanctity of marriage needs to be a top priority for the individuals. Both partners need to understand the significance of their decision.

When I was Governor of Arkansas we implemented a Covenant Marriage option, whereby the soon-to-be-husband and wife agree to structured pre-marital counseling as well as mutually deciding there will be significantly fewer grounds for divorce. Essentially it is a prenuptial agreement, where instead of the traditional form that people sign into with anticipation their marriage will not succeed, the covenant marriage is where people sign onto it with hopes of doing everything they can to preserve their marriage. They not only want to take the necessary steps before they commit, but make sure they exercise all possible avenues before even considering a divorce. The mutual consent divorce would be a good place for many states to start. It would make it that much harder for one individual to selfishly decide to end their marriage.

McManus understands the essential need for society to make lasting marriages a priority and details the vital steps to help make this happen. I applaud his stance on marriage and thank him for his commitment to moving this country forward.

Mike Huckabee, Aug 15, 2008
www.mikehuckabee.com

Introduction: How To Cut America's Divorce Rate In Half

By Mike McManus

On August 16, 2008, Dr. Rick Warren hosted a "Civil Forum on the Presidency" at Saddleback Church with Presidential nominees Barack Obama and John McCain. Dr. Warren is America's most renowned pastor, due to his authorship of *The Purpose-Driven Life,* which has sold 40 million copies, second in sales only to the Bible.[1]

In advance of the event Dr. Warren said the Forum would give American voters a more thorough understanding of the "faith, values, character, competence, leadership convictions and worldview" of both nominees.

Therefore, I submitted two questions for Dr. Warren to ask the candidates regarding what might be done to cut the divorce rate – an issue that would, indeed, test their "faith, values and character." Though Dr. Warren did pose questions on marriage, they focused on same-sex issues, not traditional marriage.

These were my questions, which I hope readers will take to the Presidential candidates, and also those running for state or federal offices:

- **Question #1.** Two-thirds of Americans were married in 1970, but less than half are married today. Though a divorce is opposed in four out of five cases by one spouse, it is always granted. **Should couples with children be required to obtain written mutual consent for the dissolution of their marriage if there are no allega-**

tions of major fault such as adultery or physical abuse?

- **Question #2. Should the Federal Government reduce a state's share of the $10 billion welfare surplus by 5% if it does not give both parents a voice on divorce?**

My purpose in writing this book is to provide the evidence needed to spark reform of state No Fault Divorce laws which *always* grant a divorce requested by one spouse. The current law in 49 states allows one spouse to file for a divorce on grounds of "irreconcilable differences," and obtain the divorce in every case. What's wrong with that? In 80% of the cases their spouses believe the marriage *is* reconcilable. The uniform granting of every divorce violates Constitutional guarantees of "due process of law." How can there be due process if the spouse who wants to save the marriage always loses? That is unjust as well as unconstitutional.

If children are involved, it is tragic. Children need to be brought up by their own married mother and father. The best parents are married parents. "About 28% of our nation's children – more than 20 million kids – will go to bed tonight without their father in the home. These children are much more likely to fail in school, to become pregnant as teenagers and to get in trouble with the law," asserts Professor Brad Wilcox of the University of Virginia.

Therefore, this book proposes that if there is no major fault alleged, such as adultery or physical abuse, in cases of couples who have children – that no divorce would be granted unless both the mother and father agree. This would replace No Fault Divorce with Mutual Consent Divorce in cases involving children. Key American religious and legal leaders predict this single step could cut divorce rates in half in any state which passed the reform.

Could Divorce Rates Be Cut in Half?

Dr. Richard Cizik, Vice President of the National Association of Evangelicals, asserts: "Mike McManus puts his finger on a simple but profound answer: require that in cases involving children that both parents would have to agree to a divorce, except in cases of adultery or physical abuse. **I believe this change in the law could cut the divorce rate in half.** That would spare 500,000 children from seeing their parents divorce each year, and save $50-$100 billion in taxpayer funds. This is an issue that should be taken to those running for state or federal offices in this election year."

Divorce Attorney John Crouch, President of Americans For Divorce Reform, explains why a half million marriages could be saved: "It is important to change state laws to reduce divorce. The best way is to replace No Fault Divorce with Mutual Consent in cases involving children. The couple would have to agree not only on the divorce, but the substance of what will happen afterward. The law would guide people to postpone the divorce decision until they had worked out the details of how the divorce would actually work. A large proportion of divorces would be avoided altogether, and most of the rest would be settled out of court. Divorces would be fairer to both parties with less legal fees. **I believe it could reduce divorce rates as much as 50 percent.** Changing the rules about ending a marriage would prevent a lot of marriages from breaking down in the first place. They would not only influence the decision to divorce, but the behavior and choices that lead to divorce."

If Cizik and Crouch are correct and every state passed Mutual Consent, a half million children a year would not experience their parents divorce. Over a decade, 5 million more children would be brought up in intact homes. It is hard to imagine any single step that could do more to strengthen the American family.

What Might Be the Impact?

Consider Modesto, California, where the divorce rate has been cut in half. It provides a working example of what such a dramatic change in marriage and divorce can mean in a community – to its marriages and to its children.

In 1986, ninety-five pastors, priests and one rabbi signed a *Modesto Community Marriage Policy* in which they pledged to take steps to more rigorously prepare couples for marriage, to enrich existing marriages and restore troubled ones. It was the first city in America to take such a step, as a result of a speech in which I challenged the clergy. I predicted, "If you take such steps as requiring thorough marriage preparation with every couple taking a premarital inventory and having it reviewed and discussed with a Mentor Couple over four months, I think you could slash your divorce rate in half in five years." By 2001, the divorce rate had fallen 57%. It has edged up slightly since, but in 2007 was still 46% below the 1986 rate.[2] The number of divorces fell from 1,852 in 1986 to only 1,709 in 2007, though the population nearly doubled from 307,000 to 521,000. The number of marriages jumped two-fold from 1,319 in 1986 to 2,729, though that is largely due to the population increase. Since 1986, America's marriage rate has fallen 18%, but it rose 15% in Modesto.

With more children reared in intact homes with married parents, there have been two important results for children. **School dropouts fell 19%. And teen births fell 30%, double the U.S. decline in the same years.**

A Marriage Culture Can Be Restored

1. Divorce Rates Drop

Modesto's results are not unique. Marriage Savers,® the organization my wife and I lead, has worked with more than 10,000 pastors and priests in 223 cities to create a Community Marriage Policy® (CMP).[3] An independent review of our first 114 CMPs signed by the year 2000 by the Institute for Research and Evaluation – reported that on average, divorce rates fell 17.5% over seven years.[4] U.S. divorce rates have come down somewhat. Therefore, researchers compared CMP counties with all 3,000 counties in the U.S. and found those in each state that were declining in five years prior to the CMP signing by pastors, at about the same rate. Researchers report that the divorce rates in the control counties fell 9.4% in the seven years that CMP counties dropped 17.5%, nearly twice as much. While that result was modest, the Institute estimated that 31,000 to 50,000 marriages were saved in those 114 CMP cities by the year 2001. With seven more years, and twice as many CMPs (223), perhaps 100,000 divorces were avoided, due to Community Marriage Policies.

2. Cohabitation Rates Fall

From 1990-2000, the Institute also reported the cohabitation rate fell 13.4% in CMP counties while it rose 19.2% in carefully matched control counties. ***Thus, CMP cities ended the decade with a cohabitation rate one-third lower than their counterparts*** (19.2 + 13.4 = 32.6).

3. Marriage Rates Rising

Marriage rates are rising in many of CMP cities. For example, Catholic Bishop Gerald A. Gettelfinger of Evansville, IN, wrote to thank Marriage Savers in 2006 for "helping us create a Community Marriage Policy (which has sparked) a significant 20% drop in the divorce rate. Hundreds of families have preserved marriages that would have probably ended in divorce, with untold trauma to many, particularly, their children. In addition, we are particularly proud to report that the number of marriages has risen. From 1997-2003, there were an average of only 1,143 marriages per year. But there were an average of 1,324 marriages in 2004-2005. That is a 16% increase in the marriage rate. What makes this especially important is that in the same time, the U.S. marriage rate fell by 9%."

Many people are aware that there has been one divorce for every two marriages every year since 1970.[5] "What few realize is that the marriage rate has plummeted more than 50 percent since 1970," my wife, Harriet, and I wrote in our recent book, *Living Together: Myths, Risks & Answers.*[6] "Census reports that in 1970, there were 76.5 marriages per 1,000 women. By 2005 that fell to only 38.7 marriages per 1,000. That is a 50.7 percent drop."

However, Marriage Savers' experience in creating Community Marriage Policies in 223 cities, reveals that *an initiative to cut the divorce rate can not only reduce divorce, but cohabitation as well, and can increase the marriage rate.* This is evidence that a marriage culture can be restored.

Cut Divorce Rates To Reduce Cohabitation and Increase Marriage Rates

It is reasonable to deduce from this Marriage Savers experience, that if a state's divorce rate was cut in half, its cohabitation rate would also fall, and its marriage rate would rise, rather than continue falling. A marriage culture can deteriorate – which is exactly what has occurred across this country. However deliberate action can be taken by government and by private groups such as churches to rebuild a healthy marriage culture. Any state that does so could expect its school dropouts and teen pregnancies to plunge.

Americans have bought into Hollywood's culture. The institution of marriage is viewed as increasingly unimportant. The traditional family is considered old-fashioned and irrelevant. Premarital sex, cohabitation, and having children without the protection of marriage is the norm. However, individual communities and states can plan and reverse these trends. Modesto is not the only city to cut its divorce rate in half. So did Austin, Kansas City, KS (and its suburbs), Salem, OR, Yuma, AZ, El Paso and Waxahachie, TX.

For example, in 1995, the year before Kansas City, KS adopted its Community Marriage Policy, there were 650 divorces in Wyandotte County where the city is located. By 2005 the number of divorces plunged to 196, a 70% plunge! And in suburban Johnson County, the divorces fell from 880 to 448 during those years.

On the other hand, Rev. Jeff Meyers of Christ Lutheran Church in Overland Park, KS who was the architect of the Kansas City Community Marriage Policy, tells the story of "Tom," an 18-year-old handyman, who was "abandoned in the hospital by his mother, and lived with dad until age 10 when his father did not come home one evening. Tom then moved in with a brother who put him on the street to sell drugs. He has no sense of what marriage is. He says, 'If you can take care of four women, what difference does it make?' We are losing a whole generation," asserted Meyers, "We need to draw a line in the sand quickly. The battleground is not about gay marriage. We are facing a huge breakdown of morality and of the social structure. The next wave is coming."

Evidence? As recently as 1970, 69% of Americans over the age of 15 were married. By 2007 it had plunged 20 points to 49 percent.

Marriage– Culture's Building Block– Is Crumbling

Therefore, we urge readers to ask the Presidential candidates, those running for Governor, State Legislature, State Senate, or Congress these two questions:

1. **Should couples with children be required to obtain written mutual consent for the dissolution of their marriage, if there are no allegations of major fault such as adultery or physical abuse?**

2. **Should the Federal Government threaten to reduce a state's share of the $10 billion welfare surplus by 5% if a state does not give both parents a voice on divorce?**

Why Is Divorce Law a Federal Issue?

Normally, we think of divorce law as the province of State Legislatures. However, the Judiciary Committees controlling divorce law are often 100 percent attorneys, many of whom personally profit greatly from divorce cases. Consequently, they are not interested in reforming the law.

But why should this law be left up to those who benefit financially by destroying America's marriages?

Currently, the law is rigged to destroy families, not to preserve them. Curiously, at the local level, it is ironic that the attorneys who refer to themselves as "members of the Family Bar" rarely have the interest of the family at heart. Rather they are concerned with their client who desires the divorce – not the marriage, the children or the family.

Given the iron grip of state law and the local divorce industry of those promoting divorce, the public must turn to "the Feds" to come to the rescue of the family. The Federal Government could be asked to nudge the state legislatures to do the right thing for America's fragile families. Why would the Federal Government care about this issue?

First, there is the simple justice of righting a wrong. Tens of millions of parents are divorcing rather than working out their differences which would ultimately benefit themselves and their children. Why? Because one unhappy spouse can demand a divorce and get it every time. What is called No Fault Divorce should be called Unilateral Divorce.

Second, federal action would restore a basic right in the Constitution of due process of law that has been robbed by state Unilateral Divorce Law.

Third, federal action would cut the federal deficit by tens of billions of dollars. A 2008 study, *The Taxpayer Costs of Divorce and Unwed Childbearing,* estimates the annual taxpayer cost of family fragmentation at $112 billion a year.[7] That is more than has been spent annually on the Iraq War! With fewer marriages in each generation, and more single parents, the situation will only worsen. Currently, only 44 percent of American teenagers are living with both married parents. They are much more likely to have children out of wedlock or a failed marriage.

What is at great risk today is:

- The future of the institution of marriage in America.

- The future of the most vulnerable and innocent – the children.

- The well being of the American culture.

- The crippling costs to taxpayers of broken marriages and non-marriages.

The good news is these trends can be reversed. Taxpayers want to see these costs decrease – not increase. Therefore, Marriage Savers recommends that the Federal Government pass a law that reduces the $10 billion Welfare Reform Surplus now going un-earmarked to the states – by 5 percent unless the states pass legislation that would transform No Fault Divorce in cases involving children – to Mutual Consent Divorce, granting equal consent to both parents regarding the outcome of a marriage.

That reform would redefine marriage and divorce in any state which passes such needed legislation – and ultimately to America as a whole. Just as No Fault Divorce swept through the nation in a few years, so could Mutual Consent. This is a Federal issue as well as a State issue, because most of the money to support divorced or never-formed families comes from the Federal Government.

Expect This Proposal to Be Denounced

Opponents will likely denounce this initiative. "You can't force someone to stay in a relationship," some will declare. "Marriage is not supposed to be endured; people are entitled to have joy and fulfillment. If I am unhappy, I have a right to leave."

My answer is three-fold:

- **First, marrying and having children are decisions that carry great responsibilities.** A parent's obligations are to provide for and protect their innocent children.

- **Second, research detailed in this book provides evidence that nine out of ten couples whose marriages are in crisis, if they stick together, are happy five years later.** There is a good reason why the marriage vows they professed were "for better, for worse." Many marriages get "worse." When that happens, a couple should remember the vow and work to improve their marriage.

- **Third, instead of adopting a victim mentality, realize that the problem is not exclusively a personal one.** If you are unhappily married, your parents divorced, or you received a divorce you did not want, remember that the true enemy is an unjust law that creates millions of victims every year. It is called No Fault Divorce. In cases involving children, it needs to be replaced by Mutual Consent Divorce. Divorce – an event you once thought of as a war between you and your spouse as warriors – might now be regarded as a malleable process that can be reformed to be in all of the participants' best interest – the parent, the children, the marriage and society.

ô

Chapter 1
Why is Divorce Reform Legislation Needed?

Marriage and Divorce in America

America is the most religious modern nation. Yet we have the highest divorce rate in the world.[8] Gallup Polls estimate that two-thirds of Americans are members of a church or synagogue and two-fifths attend services in any given week.[9] Yet, U.S. divorce rates are double that of Canada, France and Germany where church attendance figures are less than a quarter that of the United States[10]

Since 1970 there has been one divorce for every two marriages.[11] Though 86% of couples[12] exchange marriage vows before clergy to remain together "for better, for worse...till death us do part," and Christian marriages quote Jesus' injunction that "What God has put together, let no one put asunder" – 43 million couples divorced from 1970-2007, shattering the lives of 41 million children.[13]

Many of those children of divorce are now adults, and they are avoiding marriage because they fear divorce, having witnessed what it did to their parents. America's persistently high divorce rate has led to the disintegration of the institution of marriage, the foundation of every culture. These trends are detailed in a new book which my wife, Harriet, and I have written, *Living Together: Myths, Risks & Answers.*[14]

- **The marriage rate has plunged 50% since 1970.**[15]
  Why? Tens of millions are being diverted from marriage by cohabitation. There were 21 million never-married

Americans in 1970, but the number tripled to 60 million in 2006 at a time the population rose only 48%.

- **The cohabitation rate skyrocketed 15-fold from 430,000 in 1960 to 6.4 million in any month of 2007.** Probably 10 million cohabited in a year, while there were only 2.2 million marriages in 2007.

- **Today two-thirds of those who marry are cohabiting. They are 50% more likely to divorce than those who never lived together.**[16]

- **Out-of-wedlock births are soaring, rising 10-fold from 196,000 of cohabiting couples in 1970 to 1,954,000 in 2005.**

- **Many cohabiting couples believe they are in a "trial marriage."** That is a myth. With more than eight out of ten breaking up either before or after a wedding, they are really in a "trial divorce."

Divorce casts a long shadow across America, prompting millions to enter faux marriages, cohabitation, which many view as a logical way to test compatibility. Many mistakenly regard it as a step toward marriage. In fact, cohabitation for millions has become a substitute for marriage. Living together has resulted in tens of millions losing the opportunity to marry. Furthermore, cohabitants who do marry are also far more likely to divorce. Thus, America's high divorce rate is spawning a deepening cultural spiral. In less than two generations, the percentage of adults who are married has plunged from two-thirds (69%) in 1970 to less than half.[17]

Nothing could be more important to reversing these trends than to cut America's high divorce rate. If one could wave a magic wand, and pare the nation's divorce rate in half, 500,000 kids would not experience their parents' divorce each year. Being brought up in intact families, they would be more likely to marry and less likely to cohabit. That, in turn, would push down divorce rates even further.

No-Fault Divorce Accelerated the Divorce Rate

Why is America's divorce rate so high? In 1969 California passed the first so-called "No Fault Divorce"[18] law that was signed by then Gov. Ronald Reagan. Similar legislation pushed by divorce attorneys passed in almost every state in the early 1970's. Its intent was allegedly to reduce the conflict in divorce cases by allowing couples to divorce without proving fault – adultery, physical abuse, etc. It was a flawed premise. All divorces are inherently contentious.

In any case, look at the result. There were 639,000 divorces in 1969, the year of the first No Fault law, but 1,036,000 by 1975. Columnist Maggie Gallagher summed up many research studies by reporting, "No-fault did increase the divorce rate."[19] **That is an understatement. There was a 63% increase in divorces in only six years.** Some attribute this increase in the divorce rate to the Sexual Revolution. However, that was a movement primarily in the 1960's, when divorces did nearly double from 393,000 in 1960 to 708,000 in 1970.

No wonder that Ronald Reagan said his "greatest regret" was the signing of the No Fault Divorce Law, according to his son, Michael Reagan. A childhood victim of his parents' divorce, Michael hauntingly describes how it felt in his book, *Twice Adopted,* "Divorce is where two adults take everything that matters to a child – the child's home, family, security, and sense of being loved and protected – and they smash it all up, leave it in ruins on the floor, then walk out and leave the child to clean up the mess."

No Fault Divorce Is Really Unilateral Divorce

No Fault should be called "Unilateral Divorce" because 80 percent of divorces are unwanted by one spouse. In *Divided Families,* Frank Furstenburg and Andrew Cherlin report that "four out of five marriages ended unilaterally."[20] As the result of the "forced" nature of No Fault Divorce, a father (or mother) can lose a family, home, access to children and pay high child support. "Anyone who gets married has to worry about losing everything in a divorce," asserts John Crouch, J.D., Director of Americans for Divorce Reform. Perhaps 75 million Americans in broken homes are under court orders, which intrusively dictate terms of how each family is to live. No Fault allows one spouse to file on vague grounds of "incompatibility" even though their partner typically wants to save the marriage. The divorce is always granted.

No Fault Divorce is Unconstitutional.

That universal outcome – that every divorce is granted – violates the U.S. Constitution. Both the Fifth Amendment and the Fourteenth Amendment guarantee that "no person be deprived of life, liberty or property without the due process of law…" Yet how can there be "due process" of law if every divorce is granted? Challenges to the law's constitutionality do not succeed in state courts or even the U.S. Supreme Court. In fact, one Florida woman who tried to challenge her divorce on grounds that it violated her constitutional rights was fined $15,000 for "dragging her feet." (See her story on page 31).

Consider what Chief Justice John Marshall wrote in an 1819 case, which is eerily prescient:

> *When any state legislature shall pass an act annulling all marriage contracts, or allowing any party to annul it without the consent of the other, it will be time enough to inquire whether such an act be unconstitutional* [21]

Presumed Guilty

Imagine yourself as a defendant in a lawsuit. In court, the judge carefully considers statements made by the plaintiff, but disregards even your most passionate defense. You are presumed guilty. Is this a court found in some foreign country? No. This is how no-fault divorce courts operate in 49 American states...

"Critical legal protections safeguarding marriage contracts remain in place in the Empire State, while divorce courts in all other states operate in a profoundly unjust and unconstitutional manner. A New Yorker can still oppose a divorce, ask that the charges be proven, and take the case to a trial before a jury. If (no-fault) becomes New York law, defendants in no-fault divorce cases won't be able to compel plaintiffs to prove what they've claimed, and defendants will lose their constitutional rights to a jury.

"In no-fault divorce the plaintiff wins almost without exception. A defendant can't raise a legally recognized defense during the proceedings. Even an accused child molester is afforded that legal protection! If one spouse wants a divorce for any reason, the state dissolves the marriage contract, regardless of the other spouse's wishes. The plaintiff/spouse wanting the divorce needs only say in court, "Your Honor, the marriage is irretrievably broken."

"And what does irretrievably broken mean? Since these words have been used to dismantle millions of American families in no-fault divorce pleadings over the past 35 years, you might be shocked to learn that the legal profession doesn't have a consensus definition of the term irretrievably broken that is objective and measurable. Is it not, therefore, judicially unconscionable for judges in no-fault cases to make subjective judgments invalidating marriage contracts based on the claim of only one spouse?

"But what about wedding vows?" you might ask. What about them? In no-fault divorce, vows don't matter...

...the legal contracts couples enter into upon marriage won't be worth the paper on which they are written. Wedding ceremony phrases like "as long as we both shall live," will be rendered judicially meaningless. If no-fault divorce becomes New York law, the legal safeguards for marriage will be as protective as a screen door in a hurricane."

Rev. Gary Ciesla
From a column published in The New York Times, 4/12/08

A History of No Fault Divorce

Although state legislatures write marriage and divorce laws, they often use already-drafted laws from the National Conference of Commissioners on Uniform State Laws. Its work includes the Uniform Commercial Cost, the Uniform Partnership Act and the Uniform Probate Code.[22] In 1965 the Commissioners announced they were going to draft a new divorce law, a "blueprint for the states" which they called "The Uniform Divorce Project." By 1968, the Ford Foundation made a grant to staff the project. The stated goal of the Model Law was "to strengthen and preserve the integrity of marriage and to safeguard meaningful family relationships."

Their efforts, however, produced just the opposite impact. Essentially, they stripped the judge of any "judicial discretion," in divorce cases. Any person who filed for a divorce got one regardless of circumstances. The only thing that made the "Uniform Divorce" proposal uniform is that the divorce would always be granted. A California State Supreme Court Associate Justice wrote a protest to the Commission: "I respectfully submit that if marriage is to be terminable by unilateral action without any judicial determination that the marriage is in effect dead, then the proceeding has no business in a court of law and should be relegated to a ministerial function in the marriage license bureau."[23]

"There were no empirical studies to support the need for this policy-shift and the inter-disciplinary professionals that were invited to be 'advisors' and 'consultants' on the Project were marginalized or ignored."[24] "During their law-drafting sessions, the Commissioners even joked about how much of their product resembled Russia's system of Post Card divorce (See an inside account written by a Russian woman, published in the Atlantic Monthly in 1926 on www.uniformdivorce.com.)[25]

When No Fault was being considered in state legislatures, virtually no religious leader testified because they were unaware that such a momentous change was being considered. The United States Conference of Catholic Bishops and the National Association of Evangelicals certainly would have opposed it. When No Fault was considered in Florida, only a few minor changes were made in the Uniform Divorce Project's proposal. Furthermore, it took only two weeks from the end of their floor debate in 1971 to the implementation of the law, even though work was not finished on the national draft of the law. The American Bar Association did not approve it until 1974. No Fault Auto Insurance has been a success, but No Fault Divorce has bombed and needs to be replaced.

Ten Well-Kept Secrets of No Fault Divorce

Judy Parejko, author of *Stolen Vows: The Illusion of No Fault Divorce and the Rise of the American Divorce Industry*,[26] and a contributor to the www.uniformdivorce.com website, notes that few people can adequately describe what No Fault Divorce really is or how it works. Ask a lawyer, and what you will hear is that it's a "mutual" process that preserves privacy. Or they declare that it means "Nobody is at fault," or it "prevents needless conflict." In truth, however, very few couples end their marriage in a mutually satisfying way. *The law actually promotes conflict.*

In fact, this question must be asked: "What was being purposely concealed about No Fault Divorce when it was being adopted by nearly every state in the 1970's?" Ms. Parejko and Dr. Michael Ross, President of a Catholic group working to strengthen marriage, "Defending Our Father's House," reveal **Ten Secrets of No Fault Divorce:**

1. **It is still a 'lawsuit'** – one party is suing the other – even though they changed the name of the legal action to 'petition.' The plaintiff was re-named the 'petitioner' and the

defendant became the 'respondent' but a 'hearing' is still required – which is a sham.

2. **The U.S. Constitution requires that the party filing a lawsuit give a reason a "claim."** However, In No Fault, there is no claim, no 'cause of action.' It's a lawsuit without any real 'grounds.' The sole legal ground, 'irretrievable breakdown,' is merely *symbolic*.

3. **When a party is sued on any other issue, there are allowable 'defenses.'** No Fault does not allow them. That means the defendant *always* loses. Again, that is unconstitutional. We are guaranteed the right to a defense in a lawsuit.

4. **Without the two essential elements of a lawsuit – a 'cause' and a 'defense' – there's no 'case in controversy.'** This means the court process exists only for the sake of appearances – and simply put, is a *'fraud.'*

5. **The judge's role is *'ministerial'* (similar to a clerk in a state motor vehicle department).** There's no 'judicial discretion' because the 'judgment' is an 'automatic outcome.' The judge's involvement is for appearance's sake – and for enforcement of 'state authority' (ensuring the 'automatic outcome' of the law.)

6. **The party who has 'unclean hands' can be the one filing for the lawsuit, and often is set aside.** The adulterer, not the innocent spouse, is often filing for divorce. When 22 states eliminated any "fault-based divorce" from the law (see details below), they actually encouraged marital misconduct.

7. **No Fault was deceptively sold as a 'mutual agreement' process** – and most people still believe this is how it works: that both parties sign an 'agreement.'

8. **The State is not neutral** – it always takes the side of the one filing the divorce lawsuit (the 'petitioner').

9. **No-fault divorce works like the 'takings' doctrine** – with the State having the power of eminent domain over the benefits of marriage, such as health insurance, etc., are 'taken' without due process, purportedly for the Public Good.

10. **The State's police powers can be deployed** (and commonly are) to ensure the divorce takes place and to enforce the resulting court orders (child support, custody, etc.). A spouse that tries to preserve the marriage can be sanctioned with fines or jail for 'dragging their feet.'

11th Secret of No Fault:
Adultery & Abuse Are Not Grounds for Divorce

To the ten Secrets of *No Fault,* I would add an 11th. In 22 states such as Florida, Wisconsin and Michigan, one can no longer sue on grounds of fault – that your spouse committed adultery, was physically abusive, was imprisoned on conviction of a felony, etc. The only grounds on which a divorce can be granted is the "irretrievable breakdown" of the marriage. This was another recommendation of the Uniform Divorce proposal, accepted by nearly half of the states. In such states, it will not be sufficient to reform No Fault Divorce, but it will be necessary to re-establish traditional fault grounds. Those 22 states without traditional grounds for divorce are AZ, CA, CO, DE, DC, FL, HI, IA, KS, KY, MI, MN, MO, MT, NE, NV, NC, OH, OR, WA, WI ,WY.

A Divorced Man's View

Billy Miller of Alexandria, LA, who was divorced against his will expresses a righteous anger against No Fault:

"Under current No-Fault divorce laws, a divorce is granted to the first one who files EVERY TIME. You never hear a judge say, 'Divorce de-

nied.' The judge does not need to hear any accusation of wrong-doing and proof. The one who does not want the divorce [the Dads, 80% of the time] *is never permitted to challenge the divorce. A complaint can be made, but it has no effect on the results: 'Divorce granted.'*

"For the one not wanting the divorce it is NO voice, NO choice, and NO appeal. It is a done deal BEFORE court convenes. It is a foregone conclusion that the divorce WILL be granted.

- *NO obligation of contracts.*

- *NO due process [hearing what you did wrong, with proof, and legal objections, with judge's decision, and right to appeal].*

- *NO equal protection under the law.*

- *NO trial by jury of peers, which is permitted in all cases EXCEPT DIVORCE.*

"No-Fault divorce simply casts an illusion of judicial process. It is merely the 'entry ticket' by which the Courts and the state take over the family. There is NO DEFENSE against a No-Fault divorce, which is a clear and undeniable discrimination against those who do not want one."

Impact on Children

Those who suffer the most from divorce are innocent – the children. "Children without fathers, or whose parents float in and out of their lives after divorce, are the most precarious little boats in the most turbulent seas," wrote then First Lady Hillary Rodham Clinton in her book, *It Takes A Village* (p. 40). "Recent studies demonstrate convincingly that while many adults claim to have benefited from divorce and single parenthood, most children have not. Children living with one parent or in stepfamilies are two to three times more likely to have emotional and behavioral problems as children living in two-parent families... A parent's remarriage often does not seem to better the odds."[27]

For example, children of divorce are three times as likely to be expelled from school or to get pregnant as an unwed teenager as a child from an intact home. They are five times more likely to live in poverty, *14 times more likely to by physically abused, and are 2 to 12 times as apt to be incarcerated,* according to a report of the Heritage Foundation, "The Effects of Divorce on America" by Pat Fagan and Robert Rector. [28]

One man told me, "Divorce has been a train wreck in my life. My parents divorced, and my father disappeared afterwards. I did not know what a father or a husband looked like. When I married, we had three children. I admit I had a drinking problem. My wife forced a divorce against my will, and I lost everything — my business, a million dollars in costs to fight for custody of my kids, and she sent me to jail. This so destroyed our kids that my son became an armed robber and ultimately burned down a house killing two people. My daughter ran off with a boyfriend who flips hamburgers, and is only living with him. My other daughter is now institutionalized."

Between Two Worlds

Of course, most children of divorce do not become criminals or dropouts. However, even those who averted such calamity suffered intensely. There is no better book to understand the impact of divorce on average kids than *Between Two Worlds: The Inner Lives of Children of Divorce* by Elizabeth Marquardt.[29] Here is her opening paragraph:

> *"I am seven years old and climbing the jungle gym outside my school when I overhear two mothers, standing nearby. One says, 'Kids with divorced parents are kicked back and forth like a football.' The image grabs me. In this small, rural community, I had never heard anyone talk about divorce, even though my own parents had separated when I was two years old and divorced a year later. The divorce was a silent fact of my life, unnoticed by other kids, mentioned by adults only when they*

asked me how my father was doing when I came back from visiting him. Kicked back and both like a football..."

Judith Wallterstein, who followed the impact of divorce on 60 families with 100 kids over 25 years and wrote a landmark book, *The Unexpected Legacy of Divorce*,[30] wrote a Foreword to Marquardt's book. She notes that Elizabeth's parents remained civil to each other, and tried to work together on her behalf. Nevertheless, "she looks back with deep sorrow on a difficult childhood and a bewildering adolescence. These young adults recall how strange their childhoods seemed as they tried to remain connected with two homes, two parents who presented them with sharply different ideas and divergent values and eventually, as parents remarried, two new families. The author speaks of how often she felt cut in half as she tried to bridge two worlds that spun further away from each other with each advancing year. Despite her eventual successes, she remains haunted to this day by memories of how hard she had to work to keep her balance in life and how lonely she so often felt. Like several children in my studies who told me poignantly, 'The day they divorced was the day my childhood ended.'"

Cost of Divorce

A new study, *The Taxpayer Costs of Divorce and Unwed Childbearing,* provided the first rigorous estimate of the cost to taxpayers, which it calculated to be at least $112 billion a year. [31]

The thorough study was developed by the Institute for American Values, the Institute for Marriage and Public Policy, and the Georgia Family Council and Families Northwest. It includes the public cost of welfare (Temporary Assistance to Needy Families or TANF), Food Stamps, Housing Assistance, Medicaid, State Children's Health Insurance Program, Child Welfare programs, Women, Infants and Children assistance, Low Income

Home Energy Assistance, Head Start, School Lunch and Breakfast programs and part of the Justice System costs. It includes federal, state and local costs of these programs, and provides the first assessment of these costs at both national levels and for each state. The study provides detailed data for all states. It offers evidence based on many studies that "Marriage Reduces Poverty." This *Taxpayer Costs of Divorce* study thus cites evidence that could be persuasive with state legislators regarding the need to reform No Fault Divorce laws which are needlessly destroying many marriages where there is no abuse, adultery or other major faults – that also costs taxpayers tens of billions.

What's particularly significant is that the study documents that **reducing family fragmentation by even 1% would save taxpayers $1.1 billion.** State legislators are always looking for ways to reduce the costs of government to taxpayers. Reforming Divorce is one sure way to do it.

However, the *Taxpayer Costs* study of family fragmentation is very conservative in its estimates. It does not include No Child Left Behind which is $24.4 billion federal subsidy to public schools of providing remedial help for children from broken homes, for example. And only 8.7% of the cost of prisons and police are counted, for example, although the report states that 56.4% of inmates are from broken homes. Most importantly, the study unaccountably ignored the $40 billion cost of the Earned Income Tax Credit, three-fourths of which is paid to low income single parents. These additional costs likely push the total public cost of Divorce and Unwed Childbearing to the $200 billion level. (This figure, of course, does not count the private costs to individuals of attorneys and court fees.)

Stephen Baskerville Overcame Divorce Trauma

When Stephen Baskerville, Ph.D. was working as a young professor at Howard University earning $35,000 a year a decade ago, his wife divorced him against his will. He had to pay so much in child support that he had to move back into his mother's home to survive. What was more shocking was how the court controlled his life. He could only see his children every other weekend. If he went to a child's school play, he could lose even that meager opportunity. Rather than focus on his personal situation, however, he began researching what it means to be at the mercy of a divorce industry that rationalizes confiscating children from their parents. He wrote a major book in 2007, *Taken Into Custody: The War Against Fathers, Marriage, and the Family*, and has been on scores of radio shows about it. I asked him to write a brief summary of how the system works, which follows.

Divorce Licenses Unprecedented Government Intrusion

Most Americans would be deeply shocked if they knew what goes on today under the name of divorce. Indeed, many are devastated when they discover that they can be forced into divorce by procedures entirely beyond their control. Divorce now licenses unprecedented government intrusion into family life and punitive measures against parents who have done nothing legally wrong, including the power to sunder families, seize children, loot family wealth, and incarcerate parents without trial. Comprised of family courts and vast, federally funded social work bureaucracies that wield what amount to police powers, the divorce machinery has become the most repressive sector of government ever created in the United States and today's greatest threat not only to the family but also to constitutional freedom.

Today the most destructive aspect of the divorce machinery is what governs custody of children. Though obfuscated with legal jargon (losing "custody"), what it means is that a legally unimpeachable parent can be arrested for seeing his own children without government authorization. Following from this, he can be arrested for not following a variety of additional judicial directives that apply to no one but him. He can be arrested for domestic violence or child abuse, even if no evidence is presented that he has committed any. He can be arrested for not paying child support, even if the amount is not possible for him to pay (and may exceed his salary). He can even be arrested for not paying an attorney or a psychotherapist he has not hired. Once arrested, the parent is summarily jailed. There is no formal charge, no jury, and no trial.

Why do we hear almost nothing about this? Aside from media that sympathize with the divorce revolution, the multi-billion dollar divorce industry also commands a huge government-funded propaganda machine that has distorted our view of what is happening.

The growth of the divorce machinery during the 1970s and 1980s generated a series of hysterias against parents and especially fathers so hideous and inflammatory that few dare question them or defend those accused: child abuse and molestation, wife-beating, and nonpayment of "child support." Each of these hysterias has been propagated largely by feminists, bar associations, and social work bureaucracies, whose federal funding is shared with state and local law-enforcement officials. Yet it is not clear that these nefarious figures are other than bogeymen created by divorce interests.

Americans have been seriously misled about the implications of unilateral divorce. What media accounts facetiously laugh off as an amusing "battle of the sexes" is in fact a lethal political machinery. Its dynamic pervades, visibly or invisibly, every American and Western family. Its impersonal logic operates beyond the understanding of even those who participate in it. Its ruthless dynamic exploits men, women, and above all children. And its fallout is poverty, hate, violence, and prison.

Stephen Baskerville, Ph.D. Associate Professor of Government Patrick Henry College. Author, *Taken Into Custody: The War Against Fathers, Marriage, and the Family* (Cumberland House, 2007)

Public Support for Divorce Reform

Another significant resource to Reform Divorce, that will matter to politicians is that according to a TIME/CNN poll, the public agrees by nearly a 2-1 margin, that it should *"be harder than it is now for married couples with young children to get a divorce"* (61% to 35%).[32] The highly respected pollster George Gallup, Jr. told me that this has been a consistent public opinion dating back to the late 1940's when the question was first asked.[33]

One of the criticisms of Mutual Consent is that it will "lock people into unhappy marriages." As one critic put it, "You can't force people to stay in a marriage that they want to leave." This is beside the point when children are involved, because those children deserve the best possible future – which is to grow up with their married parents. It also silences the parent who does not want a divorce, unfairly removing a voice in fighting for the marriage. Both parents are supposed to provide a safe and healthy environment for their children to grow and thrive.

Those who file for divorce seem to forget that the vows taken in most marriages are "for better for worse, for richer for poorer, in sickness and in health." There are times in every marriage that are "worse," but those times will improve in nine out of ten cases, according to research by Linda Waite at the University of Chicago.[34]

Most Marriages in Crisis are Restored

"How many unhappy couples turn their marriages around?" ask Dr. Waite and Maggie Gallagher in their book, *The Case for Marriage*[35] "The truth is stunning: 86 percent of unhappily married people who stick it out find that, five years later, their marriages are happier, according to an analysis of the National Survey of Families and Households by Linda Waite for this book." This is evidence that millions of divorces, which are being forced upon unwilling spouses, are needlessly destroying marriages that could thrive with a little TLC (tender, loving care).

Remember that statistic: *86 percent of unhappily married people are happy five years later* – an important fact to remember when your friends are considering divorce.

Two Case Studies

1. "**Diane Hopkins-Jones**," a clinical psychologist, married in 1988 in a church. She says, "I don't believe in divorce, especially when you have children. You need to work through your conflicts." Professionally, Diane helps couples and individuals resolve conflict. "So my beliefs are professional and personal, that conflict can be resolved, especially when there are children. In fact you have a moral responsibility to resolve them. The optimum chance for a child's healthy development and spiritual growth is by having a good enough marriage modeling experience."

However, after 17 years of marriage, Diane's husband filed for divorce in 2004. Why? Twelve years ago he wanted to move, but she did not, which he wasn't able to forgive. Nor was she able to teach him conflict resolution skills. He fled rather than talk through issues. In addition, he had extra marital affairs, which led them to seek a marriage counselor, who also failed to teach them how to argue respectfully. Diane was never thinking about divorce, which she felt was "not an option." She was unprepared for how shocking the divorce process was.

"You get served a summons that a lawsuit has been filed against you, and you have 20 days to respond or you stand to lose your property and your children. If you want the state to hear your side of the case you must respond within 20 days. I was shocked. Why? "I never thought he would take this to that level." She also found the experience "surreal." "I had to go to a 'family attorney' which is a joke. Why call it a 'family attorney,' when what you are doing is escalating the situation? A 'family attorney' would presumably try to preserve the family. No, what they say is, 'You can not stop the divorce. This is a No Fault state, and you can't defend your marriage.'"

In her State of Florida, she found the courts want to expedite the process. "You don't know what hit you and are not able to think clearly," she recalls. "You are under pressure to through the divorce conveyor. You are divorced before you have a chance to understand it. As the respondent, I found there is no person in the yellow pages who will truly represent you. I interviewed 200 attorneys in Florida and asked if they would defend my marriage. The petitioner's attorney says, "It is a No Fault State, which means it is all over. You will get the divorce. The guidelines in most states are 90 days for an uncontested divorce, or 180 days if contested. I found that every single attorney has only one job and that is to get the people divorced."

Diane decided she would not contest the money or split of property, but "I am contesting the issue of "irretrievable break-down." My marriage is not irretrievable." However, she went through five attorneys before one was willing to take the case. As she sat outside the office of the first one, "I remember before I met her my feeling was that my civil rights are being violated. On my day off I am forced to go to an attorney office against my will. Marriage has been known to be a relationship; it is more than a contract. It is a religiously protected entity under the First Amendment. I had a religious marriage in a church that opposes all divorces." However, "The state is not only denying me my right to my religious marriage, which says there is no divorce, but also denies my right to due process because the petitioner always wins the lawsuit. You are denied your defense to the lawsuit. They abolished all defenses, so you can never defend against a lawsuit. The 14th Amendment and the 5th Amendment say that I have a right to 'due process,' an opportunity to be heard, and that you have a right have defense to the law suit. In reality, however, a respondent in a lawsuit is never heard because every single divorce is granted."

Diane recalls, "I was shocked, depressed, I could not function very well. I was crying and sad for months. It was unimaginable." Complicating matters, her husband continued living in the house. "He did not have a place to live. I thought it was a good idea for him to stay. We lived as husband and wife, sleeping in the marital bed for 15 months, having parties and living as if the filing had never occurred. Ironically, however, he had sworn under oath that the marriage is irretrievably broken, which the Supreme Court has defined as a marriage which is 'a hollow sham.'"

What's was particularly shocking to Diane was how the court treated her. After seven months with one attorney "who could not defend my marriage, and was trying to get me divorced, I fired her. I hired a second attorney, who promised he would challenge the constitutionality of the law, but the judge would not hear it. On Dec. 6, 2006 at an evidentiary hearing, my constitutional attorney cancelled a deposition because he had another case. The judge said, 'I am sanctioning her $15,000 because she is dragging her feet.'"

Diane paid a $15,000 fine for challenging the constitutionality of her divorce, and is appealing her case to the Florida Supreme Court, though the odds of success are tiny.

2. **"Dr. Peter Hopkins,"** 51, a physician whose parents divorced, grew up in a poor family in New York City. His mother suffered depression, and was unable to care for her children. Older siblings were placed in a homeless shelter while Peter and a sister were first put in a Catholic orphanage and later foster care. He put himself through college and medical school where he met his future wife. "I came to marriage with a tremendous hope for a lifelong marriage, eager to be a parent," he recalls.

They had three children who are now 17, 14 and 10. However, 10 years into the marriage, communication between them began to break down. His wife also came from a broken family. (Adult children of divorce are more likely to divorce themselves.) The couple tried to save their marriage by going to many pastors and counselors over three years, but got no help. His wife filed for divorce in 2002 and won custody of the children. It is important to note that Peter did not want the divorce. (That desire to remain married is shared by four of five spouses who experience divorce, researchers assert).

He was so determined to "remain in the lives" of his children, that he spent $250,000 on attorney's fees to get that access. He was forced to liquidate his retirement to do so, taking a 50% cut due to taxes, making his real cost nearly $500,000. That does not count the costs of various experts paid to testify on his behalf in court. The result is that he gets the kids for 48 hours every other weekend, plus one weekday each week, alternate holidays and for four weeks in the summer, while she flies regularly with the kids to visit a boy friend on the weekends. He would rather have saved his marriage, but the law makes that impossible. Every person who files for divorce gets it. Yet the cost in legal fees in the fight for access to children can be staggering.

Summary

No Fault Divorce makes marriages little more binding than cohabitation in terms of permanence. What was willingly entered into by two people can be terminated by either partner without the other's consent. No Fault is the major reason the number of divorces shot up from 639,000 in 1969 to 1,036,000 in 1975. Every year since, more than a million couples divorce annually, mostly on No Fault grounds. The marriage rate has plunged 50% since 1970, but the divorce rate has come down very modestly, because cohabitation creates weaker marriages that divorce at a rate that is 50% higher than those who remained apart.[36]

Sadly, No Fault has been exported from the United States to Europe and other countries. However, because Unilateral Divorce destroys too many marriages, shattering families, the building block of every culture, European couples who want a divorce must live separately for a long time – two years in France, three in Germany before a divorce is granted. By contrast, most U.S states allow a divorce after living separately for six months or less. Some, like Alabama, require only a month of living apart, or two months in Texas (which no longer even bothers to count the number of divorces granted, like California and Indiana). Such states experience divorce rates that are double that of others, such as Maryland where couples must live apart for a year if the divorce is uncontested, and two years if it is contested. That longer time allows for more reconciliation. France and Germany's even longer periods of required separation allows even more time for couples to resolve their differences, resulting in a divorce rate that is half that of the United States.

᠊ᢒᡐ

Chapter 2
What Is Divorce Reform?

Replace No Fault Divorce with Mutual Consent

The current law, called No Fault Divorce, or divorce on grounds of "irreconcilable differences," in reality is Unilateral Divorce in which one spouse can force divorce on an unwilling partner. That is what happens in 80 percent of cases, according to Frank Furstenberg and Andrew Cherlin, authors of *Divided Families.*[37] They argue that it is unfair to the spouse who does not want the divorce, who believes that the marriage is reconcilable. Although No Fault is less harmful to couples without children, 70% of divorces do involve a child.

There are a million divorces a year shattering the lives of a million kids. Parental divorce was devastating for the 41 million children who witnessed it since 1970. These children are much more likely to commit suicide, drop out of school and to become pregnant or delinquent. Indeed, as noted earlier, they are up to 12 times as apt to be incarcerated.[38] If a couple has children, their obligation to them should take precedence over a personal desire by one parent to abandon the marriage. Therefore, only if both parents agree to a divorce, should a marriage be terminated.

Marriage Savers[39] proposes a major reform: **replace No Fault with Mutual Consent if the couple has children.** However, it should be noted that this is a limited reform in two respects:

1. In marriages without children, either spouse could file for a No Fault Divorce.

2. If one spouse alleges a major fault, such as abuse, adultery, conviction of a felony or desertion – traditional grounds for divorce would apply. However, those traditional grounds would have to be added back to the law in 22 states which eliminated them in creating No Fault: AZ, CA, CO, DE, DC, FL, HI, IA, KS, KY, MI, MN, MO, MT, NE, NV, NC, OH, OR, WA, WI ,WY.

In other words a father would have to agree to the divorce that his wife, the mother of their children, may want. Or a mother would have to agree with her husband, the children's father, who wants the divorce. Without that consent, there would be no divorce.

Mutual Consent has been introduced in several state legislatures (New Mexico, Utah, Michigan and Virginia), but has not been enacted into law yet. Here are some examples of the legislation:

The Virginia bill (2008): States that No Fault divorce "shall not apply if

- there are minor children born of the parties born of either party and adopted by the other, or adopted by both parties, and

- either party files a written objection to the granting of a divorce…"

The Utah bill (2005:) Provides that a divorce may not be granted on the grounds of irreconcilable differences if:

- "there are living minor children of the marriage;

- "the parties have been married ten years or longer; or

- "one of the spouses contests the action.

The New Mexico bill (2003): Limits the reliance on incompatibility as grounds for divorce "Unless there is mutual consent based on both parties agreeing that incompatibility exists or the district court funds that domestic abuse…has occurred and has entered an order of protection pursuant to the provisions of that act."

The Michigan bill (2008): This bill is sponsored by Rep. Fulton Sheen, a grand nephew of Bishop Fulton Sheen, with a number of sponsors which seems promising. HB 5761 states that citizens can file in circuit court for a no-fault divorce if either of the following apply:

- There are no minor children and wife is not pregnant

- The divorce filing contains a statement signed by both husband and wife agreeing to a no-fault divorce

If neither point applies, then a divorce may be filed only by alleging one or more of six fault grounds (adultery, physical abuse, etc).

The Law's Bias Shifts From One Who Wants Out To Children

At present the law favors the spouse least committed to the marriage, the person filing for divorce. Mutual Consent would shift the bias toward the spouse who wants to preserve the marriage, toward the children, and to preserving the family. It would give that spouse leverage to fight for the marriage. Why? The state has an interest in the future of those children and knows that in most cases those children are best brought up by their own married parents. Such children perform better in school and are less likely to become pregnant out of wedlock or delinquent. The principle here is clear and profound: *What was entered into by two people should not be terminated unless both spouses agree, if children are involved.*

Rather than a return to the former system, in which all divorces were granted only on grounds of fault, the preferred goal is to give both parents of children under 18 an equal voice in the future of their relationship with each other and their children.

Why? Studies indicate that most divorces are not over substantial issues. One such study estimates that severe conflict is present in only 30 percent of the cases,[40] according to a study reported in *The Case for Marriage* by Linda Waite and Maggie Gallagher.[41]

Mutual Consent Would Spark Negotiation

As a practical matter, Mutual Consent would spark a negotiating process. Critics say that changing the law would imprison people in unhappy marriages. On the contrary, it would simply give bargaining power to the spouse trying to save the marriage. That is a matter of equity, of simple justice, of respect to the other parent of the children and to the children themselves.

In the era before No Fault, a husband might ask for a divorce but his wife could say, "No, I won't agree to it. We have two kids. You made a vow before God 'for better for worse.' We have been married for 13 years and have two kids, who deserve to be brought up by their married mother and father.'" He might then reply, "But I am in love with my secretary, and I could run off with her, but I am trying to be fair to you. I will give you my equity in our house." She could reply, "But I don't earn enough to make the mortgage payments. I could sue you for divorce on grounds of adultery, but I will not. Give her up and let's seek help and try to heal our marriage." In this scenario, the spouse who did not want the divorce has leverage in denying a divorce to the spouse who does.

The husband then has to make a decision – whether to give up his lover and work to improve the marriage or offer alimony in addition to the house.

Five Societal Gains of Mutual Consent

Five major societal gains would result from Mutual Consent replacing No Fault:

1. **Fewer divorces:** Experts such as John Crouch, a divorce attorney and Director of Americans for Divorce Reform, estimates that if Mutual Consent replaced No Fault Divorce, the divorce rate could fall as much as 50%. Why? "Making marriage a more reliable contract will change the incentives that affect spouses' behavior and decisions throughout the marriage." It is significant that America's religious leaders agree that the reform could cut the divorce rate in half, such as Richard Cizik, Vice President of the National Association of Evangelicals and Catholic Bishop Gerald Gettelfinger.

2. **Fairer divorces:** In the case described above, the spouse trying to save the marriage can gain economic advantages through a negotiation process. This kind of divorce would leave fewer women and children destitute.

3. **Friendlier divorces:** Couples would have to negotiate first instead of resorting to ugly, expensive courtroom battles. More cases would be resolved by negotiation, collaborative divorce, or mediation, rather than judges with exorbitant fees paid to divorce attorneys. Studies indicate that when people make their own decisions in mediation or negotiation, they are less likely to go back to court later to change or enforce the terms of the divorce.

4. **More responsibility:** If the terms have to be agreed upon by both parties, parents will assume more responsibility to protect their children. Currently individuals decide to divorce without considering the many painful consequences: how the children's time will be divided between parents and how the family's income, property and

debt will be allocated. They frequently end up with results neither spouse expected or wanted. Having to consider these practical issues as part of the divorce process will help them realize what they're getting into before it's too late. Many will conclude it would be easier to make the marriage work than to make the divorce work.

5. **Restore Due Process of Law:** Mutual Consent would provide the "due process" of law guaranteed by the Constitution's 5th and 14th Amendments. Instead of the court rubber-stamping every divorce, the parent who refused to sign off on the divorce could stop it. That would give the spouse who wants to save the marriage a leverage sadly missing today.

For example, consider a case study of an adulterous wife who filed for divorce. Her husband, a father of children aged 4, 7 and 9, was willing to forgive her adultery if she gave up her lover. While he could file for divorce on grounds of adultery, he wanted to save the marriage and preserve the family. Current law allows unilateral divorce: therefore, he has no leverage in court to stop the divorce. If Mutual Consent were required in this case, the wife could not get divorced without her husband's consent. She would then be forced to pursue healthier options such as giving up her affair, and attend a marriage enrichment weekend for couples in crisis such as Retrouvaille with her husband. Retrouvaille restores four out of five marriages. (www.retrouvaille.org).

The Value of Restoring "Fault" to Divorce

There is a societal value to restoring fault to the law. Today, the adulterer can force the divorce on their spouse without impunity. By removing "fault" from the law inadvertently the law encourages irresponsible behavior – indeed, rewards it. Lawyers like No Fault because they don't have to do the research needed to make a case for adultery or physical abuse. However the law should not exist for the lawyers' convenience but to serve the people.

Before No Fault divorce millions of parents worked out their marital differences for the sake of their kids. More will do so in the future, but only if State Legislatures replace No Fault Divorce with Mutual Consent. Family Courts would cease to be kangaroo courts. If spouses could not unilaterally divorce each other, they would be more likely to honor their marriage vows 'till death do us part' often pledged at wedding services, and remain married.

Why should couples try to make their marriage work? *Because children need both their married mother and father.* What was entered into willingly by two people should not be terminated by one spouse who ignores the future well-being of their mate and their children. Government has an interest in the future of children as well, and knows they are best provided for with the love that only their married mother and father can offer.

Numerous studies indicate that children fare better when their parents remain married, except in the comparatively few high-conflict divorces. One of the most unsettling statistics documented in *The Case for Marriage* is that parental divorce reduces the life expectancy of their adult children by four years: "Forty-year-olds from divorced homes were three times as likely to die from all causes as forty-year-olds whose parents stayed married."[42.]

Replace Sole Custody with Shared or Equal Parenting

If there is a divorce with children, the law should replace a presumption of Sole Custody with a presumption of Joint Custody, Shared Parenting or Equal Parenting. States with the most Joint Custody enjoyed the largest drop of divorce in the 1990's. The evidence: The states which approved the strongest presumption of Joint Custody are Montana, Kansas, Connecticut, Idaho,

Rhode Island, and Alaska. Five of those states also had the largest decline in divorce rates in the 1990's: Montana, Kansas, Connecticut, Idaho and Alaska.

Why? Attorney David L. Levy, CEO of the Children's Rights Council, says, "If a parent knows that he or she will have to interact with the child's other parent while the child is growing up, there is less incentive to divorce."

The exact nature of Shared Parenting would be worked out by the husband and wife. Presumably, it would have to be a core ingredient of a Mutual Consent Divorce or one spouse would block the divorce. Most fathers would like to have a 50-50 share of time with their children or "Equal Parenting," or at least one-third time called Shared Parenting, according to John Crouch. However Sole Custody is the norm where fathers see their kids only every other weekend, minimizing their access and influence. Shared Parenting would rarely mean 50-50 split of time, but realistically might be closer to two-thirds - one-third. Some form of Shared Parenting exists in many states, such as Texas which guarantees each parent joint custody with at least one-third of the time with children. There are many ways to implement Shared Parenting:

- The wife might care for the children during the week, the father every weekend.

- In some cases, the children would stay in the same house, and the mother or father would take turns moving in and out to care for the children.

- There might be an agreement that a mother would have primary custody with young children, at very early ages, 1-12. The mother might have them two-thirds of their time, and 100% in the case of nursing infants.

- At age twelve, primary custody could shift to the father who would care for the children during the week.

In these cases, the other parent would see their children at least a third of the time. Sole Custody with one spouse having the children 12-13 out of 14 days – virtually removes millions of fathers from their parenting role. Moving out-of-state would be prohibited, unless mutually agreed upon. No parent who is fit should have less than one-third of the children's time.

John Crouch and David L. Levy estimate Shared Parenting or Equal Parenting would reduce divorce rates by 20%, part of the 50% drop predicted for Mutual Consent's impact.

Mutual Consent Would Have to Include Shared Parenting

With a Mutual Consent Requirement before a divorce was finalized, couples would have to negotiate issues ahead of time, such as whether moving out-of-state is permissible. A division of the couple's property would have to be agreed upon to make divorce affordable for each of them. Under current law, what often happens is one spouse makes a decision to divorce in the abstract, without considering the consequences regarding children, property and one's spouse.

Currently, each parent makes the divorce decision expecting to be awarded their ideal custody arrangement, instead of finding out what their spouse wants and what the courts will be likely to enforce. Mutual Consent would reverse the order of decision-making, forcing the person contemplating the divorce to consider all of the complications, and the necessity of gaining their spouse's consent. In half of the cases what is likely to occur is that the couple will decide to stay in the marriage and work to make it better.

According to Crouch, Mutual Consent would force the couple to agree not only on the divorce, but what happens afterward.

The negotiation would persuade many not to divorce at all. Most would settle out of court, in much fairer agreements and would save thousands in legal fees. Most important, he asserts that he believes **Mutual Consent "could reduce divorce rates as much as 50 percent.** Changing the rules about ending a marriage would prevent many marriages from breaking down in the first place. They would not only influence the decision to divorce, but the behavior and choices that lead to divorce."

Baskerville Predicts Cutting Divorce Rates in Half

Another expert in the field who believes the divorce rate would be cut in half is Prof. Stephen Baskerville, of James Madison University and author of the influential 2007 book, *Taken Into Custody: The War Against Fathers, Marriage, and the Family.* In an endorsement of this book, he wrote, "Divorce is the most serious force for family destruction in the Western world today, and therefore it is also the greatest threat to both civic order and freedom itself. Mike McManus's proposal for mutual consent divorce and other reforms offers the realistic prospect of reducing the divorce rate by half and of creating a needed national dialogue on this unaddressed crisis."

A Half Million Kids Spared from Parental Divorce

These reforms, if enacted nationally, could save a half million marriages a year from divorce and its shattering impact on innocent children. There are a million children affected annually by divorce. Therefore, 500,000 children would be spared from experiencing their parents divorce annually. Therefore five million more kids would remain in intact families each decade.

Taxpayers Would Save Tens of Billions

Mutual Consent would also save tens of billions of federal and state tax dollars now subsidizing divorce. How much? A recent report by the Institute for American Values, *The Taxpayer Costs of Divorce and Unwed Child Bearing*, estimates family breakdown costs $112 billion a year.[43] This figure includes the costs of welfare, Food Stamps, housing subsidies, Medicaid, school lunch and breakfast programs, day care subsidies, etc. That $112 billion is more than the annual appropriations for the Iraq War. And this figure is a very low estimate. As noted above, the estimate did not include the cost of the Earned Income Tax Credit at $40 billion yearly, nor the $24 billion cost of "No Child Left Behind" to educate those from poor families. It only counted 8.6% of court, police and prison costs, though most inmates are from failed marriages or non-marriages. I believe the total might be $200 billion.

However, if the $112 billion cost is accurate, the study estimated that even a 1% drop in the divorce rate would save state and federal taxpayers $1.1 billion. Therefore if Mutual Consent sparked a one-third reduction of divorce, taxpayers would save $36 billion a year! A 50% plunge would save $55 billion. If the $200 billion public cost of broken families is more realistic, as much as $100 billion of federal and state spending could be saved each year. Both Barack Obama and John McCain should be interested in a proposal that would radically ***reduce the deficit – while preserving families.*** Every Member of Congress or U.S. Senator – or those running against them – would find this information of keen interest.

It would be in every Governor's and Legislator's interest because the $55 billion to $100 billion savings to taxpayers would be shared by State and Federal Governments. More important, millions of children would perform academically better and would be more likely to mature into responsible citizens. Child support orders would be modified to give both parents better access to children.

Set Aside 1% of Welfare (TANF) Funding to Strengthen Marriage

Two of the purposes of the Welfare Reform Law passed by Congress in 1996 relate to marriage:

1. To prevent and reduce the incidence of out-of-wedlock pregnancies

2. To encourage the formation and maintenance of two-parent families

Another goal of welfare reform was to "reduce the dependence of needy parents on government benefits by promoting job preparation, work and marriage." The result has been a 60% drop in the numbers of families receiving public assistance. Yet, the federal law continued to give $16.5 billion block grant to the states in federal TANF (Temporary Assistance to Needy Families, what used to be called AFDC) funding. Thus, the states are getting a $10 billion bonus which I call a "Welfare Reform Surplus." Virtually none of those funds has been earmarked for marriage, except in a few states such as Texas where the Legislature set aside 1% of TANF funds to strengthen marriage.

An organization called **FAMLI** (Fatherhood and Marriage Leadership Institute) led by former HHS Deputy Assistant Secretary Chris Gersten, has promoted a "1% Solution Campaign" to win state funding for marriage strengthening programs. Its core idea is to persuade states to set aside 1% of its welfare spending (TANF) for healthy marriage initiatives. Clearly, the states have the money. A request for a 1% set-aside is a very modest goal.

Texas recently passed a law earmarking $15 million to strengthen marriage education. The Texas Health and Human Services Commission created what it calls "Twogether in Texas," which is funding a variety of healthy marriage initiatives. For example, if couples take an 8-hour premarital class that focuses on communication and conflict management skills – the state waives the normal marriage license fee, which was raised from $30 to $60. Twelve Regional Intermediaries are funding those free pre-marital education classes and other initiatives with a $950,000 per region grant for 18 months, beginning in September 2008.

Utah passed a similar 1% TANF set-aside in 2006, allocating $750,000 for a Utah Healthy Marriage Initiative, according to FAMLI. It will fund a public awareness campaign, Marriage Week activities, capacity-building including the formation of local coalitions and research.

Mississippi has set-aside $2 million of TANF funding through a series of sub-grant awards to provide marriage and relationship skills education including parenting skills, financial management and conflict resolution for non-married pregnant women and expectant fathers; pre-marital education and marriage skills training for engaged couples; marriage enhancement and marital skills training for married couples; divorce reduction programs that teach relationship skills and marriage mentoring programs using married couples as role models and mentors in at-risk communities. Priority is given to low-income families/individuals (income at or below 200% of poverty.)

The Federal Government Should Set Aside Marriage Funding?

The examples above demonstrated the viability of this idea. Therefore, why not ask Congress to consider a similar "Set-Aside off 1% of TANF's $16.5 billion, earmarked for marriage education that would provide an annual appropriation of $165 million. The Bush Administration did persuade Congress to appropriate $100 million a year to strengthen marriage in 2006, but the grants were given out on a five-year basis to few recipients. Compared to billions of dollars given to single parents and their children, the incentives to break up marriage are huge. A more appropriate set-aside might be 5% or $825 million. Presidential candidates and those running for Congress or U.S. Senate should be asked where they stand on a Federal earmarking of 5% of TANF funds not being spent on public assistance.

Marriage Savers Cut Divorce and Cohabitation Rates, Increased Marriage

Marriage Savers, the organization founded by my wife and me, has helped the clergy of 223 cities by July 2008 (more than 10,000 pastors and priests) to create "Community Marriage Policies"® that have pushed down divorce and cohabitation rates, and raised marriage rates. How? Marriage Savers trains couples in healthy marriages to become "Mentor Couples" to help other couples to prepare for, enrich and restore marriage at five stages of the marital life cycle:

1. **Rigorously prepare couples for marriage,** by requiring 4-6 months of preparation that includes taking a premarital inventory, meeting with a trained mentor couple to discuss its results and learn conflict resolution skills. Over a decade, in Harriet's and my home church, the Mentor Couples we trained prepared 288 couples for marriage. They meet with a Mentor Couple 6-7 times over 3-4 months, 55 decided not to marry, a whopping 19%. But of those who did marry, there were only 7 divorces or separations over a decade. That is a 3% failure rate over a decade, or a 97% success rate. *That is virtual marriage insurance.*

2. **Enrich existing marriages** with an affordable annual retreat at the church, using an inventory, videos, or speakers. We suggest two proven and effective ways to strengthen a church's marriages: "10 Great Dates," a DVD based marriage education program by David and Claudia Arp, in which couples come for great dates and go home with marriage skills. They meet at the church for 10 consecutive Saturday nights, watch a video date launch on a topic such as "Resolving Honest Conflict" or

"Building A Creative Love Life." Couples then go out on a 90-minute date, perhaps for dessert and coffee, to discuss that evening's theme. Each couple only needs one copy of $13 participants' book which has duplicate tear-out dating exercisees. (For more information see www.marriagealive.com). An alternative way to enrich existing marriages is to complete and discuss the marital inventory, REFOCCUS, at a weekend retreat at the church. After hearing a brief talk on an issue such as Communication or Commitment, couples respond to inventory items and compare and discuss previously unresolved issues. A REFOCCUS retreat could be scheduled in any church for Friday night and Saturday at a cost of only $15 per couple (Contact www.marriagesavers.org).

3. **Restore marriages in crisis by training** "back-from-the-brink" couples whose own marriages once nearly failed to mentor those in current crisis, saving four of five troubled marriages. Therapists save less than 20% of troubled marriages, while Mentor Couples can save 80% or more – the mirror opposite.

4. **Reconcile the separated** with a workbook course called "Marriage 911" that a spouse trying to save his/her marriage completes over a 12- week period with a Support Partner of the same gender. It is designed for those cases where one spouse is not interested in saving the marriage. Part of the course involves reading a chapter of Proverbs daily. This course costs only $28 and is successful because it helps the spouse trying to save the marriage grow in such a way that the errant spouse is attracted back in more than half the cases.

5. **Help stepfamilies succeed** by creating a Stepfamily Support Group that can save four of five marriages that typically divorce at a 70% rate. The concept is similar to

Alcoholics Anonymous, in which people who overcame their addiction – tell their stories of recovery, using the 12 steps of AA. Similarly, Stepfamily Support Groups is a peer ministry, as opposed to therapy or counseling. Five step couples are instructed how to create a Stepfamily Support Group with a kit that includes a Manual on how to organize the group, a paperback book, *Willing To Try Again* by Rev. Dick Dunn, and a CD by Rev. Dunn. Cost: $40.[44] (Contact www.marriagesavers.org)

This evidence clearly shows how a 1% set-aside of TANF funds could reduce divorce rates by even more than 50 percent drop if Mutual Consent replaces No Fault in cases involving children. If federal funding were used to create Community Marriage Policies, the local divorce rate would drop an additional 15% to 20% in seven years on top of the 50% drop due to Mutual Consent, if these cities were as successful as the average Community Marriage Policy.

છે

Chapter 3
Major Obstacles to Reforming Divorce

A Marriage Commission's Perspective

In the fall of 2007 as President of Marriage Savers,[45] I had the opportunity to serve on The Marriage Commission of Virginia organized by The Family Foundation, an affiliate of Focus on the Family. The Commission included representatives of the office of the Governor, Lt. Governor and Attorney General, noted national marriage leaders such as Maggie Gallagher, co-author of *The Case for Marriage,* John Crouch of Americans for Divorce Reform, prominent Virginia academics Brad Wilcox and Steven Nock of the University of Virginia, Bob Ruthazer of First Things First, Richmond (a Community Marriage Policy Marriage Savers helped to create), plus law professors, attorneys and therapists. After four meetings the group agreed to support replacing No Fault Divorce with Mutual Consent. However, almost no legislator was willing to introduce the legislation. When a bill was finally proposed, it never got out of committee. Why?

Ignorance & Fear

First, there is a lack of knowledge about the financial cost of divorce, and second, a fear of addressing the issue. "Legislators do not understand the issue. It was difficult to find anyone to patron the bill," says Chris Freund, V.P. of the Family Foundation. "They do not know the cost of divorce in tax dollars. The new study by the Institute for American Values will be immensely helpful in providing the precise data on billions of taxpayer dollars on the cost of marital breakup and of non-marriage."

He adds, "The bigger problem is fear, which supersedes ignorance. They are afraid of a backlash if they have anything to do
with divorce, that it will cause repercussions. There also is an as-
sumption that abuse is always included in divorce," which will
attract feminist opponents. Even though the bill as drafted clearly
excludes fault grounds, such as adultery or abuse, fear clouds
thought or reasoned analysis. Why? Freund blames America's
"libertarian spirit of live and let live. Also, so many of them have
divorced, or know people who are divorced, and its damage does
not seem that great."

Denial

If one has contributed to the demise of a marriage, there is a
natural tendency to minimize or deny the perceived consequences
to one's spouse, and especially to one's children. "Children get
over it. They are resilient," they rationalize. Really? Why then has
there been a 15-fold increase in the number of cohabiting couples, soaring from 430,000 in 1960 to 6.4 million couples in 2007?

As Harriet and I report in our new book, *Living Together:
Myths, Risks & Answers,*[46] cohabiting couples are usually children
of divorce who fear marriage because they fear divorce, having
witnessed how traumatic it was for their parents. A second large
cohort of cohabiting couples is adult children of non-marriage.
Neither group of young adults has witnessed a healthy marriage.
They know what a mother is, but more than 20 million kids do
not know what a father is like – let alone what a husband or wife
roles are. The adults who caused this trauma by divorcing their
spouse, or never marrying the other parent of their children – are
usually oblivious to the impact of their choices on the next generation. Thus, a combination of the fear of children of divorce
and the choices of their parents – make divorce a third rail that
legislators would rather not touch.

Attorneys Control Key Committees, Oppose Reform

In Virginia 100% of the legislators on key committees are attorneys, most of whom have no interest in Divorce Reform. If they are not divorce attorneys (members of the "Family Bar") who make money on divorce cases, their sympathies are with their colleagues, not with those who want to make divorce more difficult to obtain. Victoria Cobb, Executive Director of The Family Foundation (an affiliate of Focus on the Family), had introduced Mutual Consent legislation in 2007, and thought a Marriage Commission might give added weight to the cause in 2008. She had also led a successful battle to pass a Constitutional Amendment to limit marriage to a man marrying a woman. Critics of that initiative invariably said, "Gay marriage is less of a threat to marriage than divorce. Why don't you do something about that?" However, two years of Family Foundation initiatives have proven to be fruitless. Nevertheless, she will publish the Marriage Commission's report in 2008 as a constructive prod to the 2009 Legislature.

Here's how LSU Law Professor Katherine Spaht described the reluctance of the legal system to change No Fault Divorce in an article in a 2005 book by John Witte, Jr., a fellow law professor, *Covenant Marriage in Comparative Perspective:*

"Lawyers often oppose divorce reform because reform is a threat to their economic livelihood. No-fault divorce permitted family law attorneys to make money on the volume of divorces they handled and to satisfy their clients, at least parties who desire divorce. Because there is no defense to a no-fault divorce other than reconciliation, the lawyer simply completes the blank portions of a uniform pleading (petition) and files it. The lawyer need not prove facts entitling the petitioner to a divorce, which involves time-consuming discovery and the use of possibly salacious material to prove fault grounds for divorce. Without a defense to the action for divorce, the lawyer can concentrate on the more lucrative and satisfy-

ing litigation, litigation that divides the property accumulated by the couple. Unlike the former fault system of divorce there is little possibility that the client will fail to obtain the divorce judgment, so the lawyer may begin work immediately on the incidental matters dependent upon the judgment itself. Work on those incidental matters, except for child custody, ordinarily concerns money and requires hours of legal analysis for which the attorney may charge the client. In addition, the content of the law that classifies property acquired during marriage, for example, is far more intellectually engaging and interesting than having to build a case for divorce on the basis of the behavior of the client's spouse."[47]

In a small book detailing the legal profession's responsibility for no-fault divorce in California, Judy Parejko helps the reader understand how lawyers cleverly reshaped no-fault divorce legislation to eliminate the conciliation components in the bill that was introduced. She also describes the legal profession's contribution to the interpretation of irreconcilable differences as simply one spouse's desire to divorce. Her book, Stolen Vows, *makes a valuable contribution by exposing the motivations of lawyers in opposing divorce reform, whether in the form of lawyers who serve on legislative committees to which such bills are referred, or of the profession as a whole which sees its livelihood threatened by reform efforts. In the words of Indiana lawyer Brent Welke, writing to the Chairs of the Indiana Judiciary Committee, 'Please be advised that, speaking as a lawyer, I am unalterably opposed to any change in our divorce act. Our divorce act has greatly increased divorces, crime, bankruptcy and juvenile caseloads, Any change in our no-fault system would be a financial disaster for the bar and for me personally, as these type of cases comprise a majority of my practice" (in a letter from Welke).*

The Divorced Blame Their Ex-Spouse, Not the System

Four out of five people who were divorced against their will understandably blame their ex-spouse for the divorce. They never consider that the law, theoretically designed to dispense justice – unfairly does just the opposite. No Fault Divorce makes it possible for a spouse to divorce a mate unilaterally, even if the partner wants to work out differences.

Few people today remember when no one could get a divorce unless their spouse agreed to it. Mutual Consent divorce is a long-forgotten concept. The first No Fault law was signed by California Gov. Ronald Reagan in 1969 and by 1973 other states largely adopted No Fault. That was 35 years ago, long before most of today's adults were adults. The concept that the law could prevent a spouse from getting a divorce, if the couple has children is virtually unknown today. No Fault actually rewards the person with the least interest in the marriage – and penalizes the person who is trying to save it on behalf of themselves and their children. This is a not only a travesty of justice but is highly destructive to marriage, the foundation of a healthy civilized society. The bias of the law should *support* marriage – not destroy it. No wonder the percentage of American adults who are married has plunged from 69% in 1970 - to less than 50% today.[48]

A Case Study – Sam Baker

At the time of this writing, "Sam Baker" was in a divorce trial.[49] Since his wife was a stay-at-home mother, he would have been comfortable giving her half of his assets, which was $95,000. However, the judge ruled that the entire $95,000 should be given to his wife and also required him to pay many household bills. The judge also permitted her to take out $3,000 a month for support, leaving only $11,000 of the $95,000 in July, 2008. The judge allowed his wife to move into an expensive, furnished rental property owned by the couple. Sam Baker had to use IRA savings to pay a $30,000 tax bill and attorney fees of $15,000. He has been to court five times and is now representing himself since he has no money to hire a lawyer. During the trial his wife was allowed five days to testify, while he had only five hours to explain why he was trying to save a marriage of 17 years. She committed adultery, while he had remained faithful, nor was he physically abusive. They have four children aged 5, 8, 12, 15. He wants to reconcile with his wife, but has no power to do so. I asked him if he would like to see Mutual Consent replace No Fault in the law, he replied, "Absolutely. There is no justice in the present system. I want to save my marriage, but am unable to do so. And I am losing everything – my wife, children, money."

Lack of Outrage

Unfortunately, there has been no outrage expressed over the cause of America's high divorce rate, of one divorce for ever two marriages every year since 1970, which is double that of most European countries. There are probably 30 to 40 million adult children of divorce who are understandably fearful of marriage and as a result cohabit rather than marry. Few realize that cohabiting actually increases their odds of divorce, if they marry. In 2007 there were 6.4 million cohabiting couples at any moment of time, and only 2.2 million marriages all year. One direct consequence has been a ten-fold increase in the number of children living with cohabiting couples.[50] (There were only 196,000 children under 18 living with unmarried parents in 1970 but 1,954,000 in 2005.)[51]

One of the most prevalent myths widely believed by couples who are living together is that they "are in a trial marriage." As we write in *Living Together: Myths, Risks and Answers,* "They are actually in a trial divorce. The only question is will they break up before or after the wedding?" (More than half, perhaps two-thirds,[52] break up before the wedding; and of those who marry, they are at least 50% more likely to divorce than those who remained apart. More than eight of ten cohabiting relationships will fail. The pain of their parents' failed marriage or non-marriage, frequently contributes to their own inability to build a lasting marriage.

Divorce causes intense personal pain, whether one is a child of divorce or person who received an unwanted divorce. These people understandably blame the individuals who initiated the divorce. Almost no one is focused on the ultimate cause of the unwanted divorce – the No Fault system which grants every divorce filed for. Without a sense of outrage directed against an unjust law, it will never be changed.

Consequently, there is no visible remedy to the injustice impacting either the Baby Boom Generation, or their kids, the Baby Busters, sometimes called Generation X, or the "Millennial Generation."

ॐ

Chapter 4
Strategy to Reform Divorce

Create a Movement Like
Mothers Against Drunk Driving

Mothers Against Drunk Driving (MADD) is an example of the kind of citizen movement that will be needed to reform divorce laws. In 1982 when Candy Lightener's daughter was killed by a drunk driver she created MADD. Drunk driving was then considered more of a joke on late night TV shows rather than a major social problem. (Johnny Carson cracked about his DUI arrest, for example.) An initial MADD goal was to raise the age at which liquor could be bought to 21, up from 18 in many states.

When this author was an 18-year-old college student living in Connecticut, I drove to Port Chester, New York where I could buy drinks at age 18, three years below Connecticut's 21 requirement. Many kids died in accidents after getting drunk and driving home from a neighboring state. A second goal was to push down the definition of drunk driving to .08 Blood Alcohol Content (BAC). More than a half dozen states defined "drunk driving" as having .15 BAC, which is falling-down drunk, such as Massachusetts. Other states requiring a .10 BAC only gave a slap on the wrist for first convictions.

In MADD's first year, Candy Lightener met with then-Gov. Jerry Brown of California, to ask for his support. Although he was sympathetic, nothing happened. Chuck Hurley, current CEO of MADD, recalls that their first success came in 1984 when they persuaded Congress to add an amendment to the Transportation Appropriations Law that reduced a state's federal highway funding by 10%, unless they had in place or passed a state law setting 21 as the age one could buy alcohol. A wave of state legislation followed. A similar amendment in 2000 reduced highway funding by another 8% if states did not define drunk driving as .08 BAC. "When you have a formula for success, you don't change your strategy!" Hurley recently asserted.

Result: In 1982 there were 30,600 traffic fatalities due to drunk driving. By 2006, that number plunged to only 17,600.

MADD's success suggests two important strategies to spark divorce reform:

1. Create a "Citizens For Divorce Reform" movement.

2. Make cutting the divorce rate in half a 2008 Presidential Campaign Issue

Create "Citizens For Divorce Reform" (CFDR)

State divorce laws won't change until citizens concerned about divorce become incensed enough to demand reform. Attorneys dominate state Judiciary Committees, where any legislation to change marriage and divorce laws would originate. Thus far, only the marriage experts have spoken about the need for divorce reform, but legislators pay scant attention to them on such a volatile issue. They need to hear from their constituents. *Thus, the key is to create a movement of thousands of citizens willing to call up their state legislators and urge them to act.*

This author proposes creating a group like MADD called **"Citizens For Divorce Reform."** CFDR lacks the snappy acronym of MADD, but it is designed to motivate parents who had an unwanted divorce forced upon them – to stop placing all of the blame on their ex-spouses and focus instead on the law which makes divorce too easy to obtain, a belief which polls indicate is shared by 61% of Americans. George Gallup cites a consistency in public attitudes on this question going back 60 years.[53]

Polls, however, do not persuade legislators. They do indicate, instead, that there is great potential for the movement we envision. Who might be mobilized? Five groups understand the pain of divorce from first-hand experience might help create **Citizens For Divorce Reform:**

1. **Adult Children of Divorce.** As noted earlier, just since 1970, 41 million children saw their parents divorce. Perhaps another 15 million were shattered by a parental divorce between 1950 and 1970. That would yield about 35 million adult children of divorce, who would be the excellent pioneers for this movement. Many resent their parents divorce, but have not known political action was possible. Some are angry about divorce because as adult children of divorce they were deprived of a healthy marriage model, and subsequently their own marriages failed or they experienced broken cohabitation relationships. But they know nothing about the No Fault causes of divorce, nor anything about the remedies. They are the first target of this book.

2. **Adult Children of Non-Marriage.** The number of children born out-of-wedlock reached a million a year about 20 years ago, surpassing the number affected by divorce. The numbers of adult children of unwed parents are in the 10 to 15 million range. These children fare the worst in our society, and are less likely to yield many leaders for this movement, vs. children of divorce who generally grew up in middle class homes. However, there are individuals like Dr. Michael Ross, who grew up in poverty and foster homes who built a successful professional career, even though his life was shattered by an unwanted divorce. He is now leading "Defending Our Father's House," a Catholic activist group in Michigan pushing for reforming divorce law and creating Community Marriage

Policies to reduce divorce and cohabitation rates and raise marriage rates.

3.   **Victims of Divorce.** Since 80% of divorces are filed against the will of one partner, there are many hurt and angry people who might be mobilized – 43 million just since 1970. A number of the Community Marriage Policies that Marriage Savers[54] helped clergy to organize were sparked by a victim of divorce, who wanted to spare others from experiencing the same pain. They do not know anything about the unfairness of the law, but if they knew, likely they would be motivated to join this movement in many states. Undoubtedly, this is the most important constituency for **Citizens For Divorce Reform.** A parent who has a divorce forced upon them often unwittingly relinquishes far more than his or her marriage. They lose their home, regular access to their children, and are often forced to pay exorbitant child support costs. Even when it was their errant spouse who was unfaithful to the marriage covenant, the person who files for divorce – gains economic advantage and usually wins custody of the children. Our goal is to re-direct that anger fired by injustice from the ex-spouse toward the law that always grants a divorce.

4.   **People who work with divorcing families.** Many influential people in the community are in a position to witness the carnage that occurs in divorce cases and how it affects parents and children. Judges, therapists, teachers, lawyers, clergy, social workers, and law enforcement officers are among the people who have contacted Marriage Savers wanting to do something to reduce divorce, including changing the law. In each of these professions, most people probably do not question the current system, or have not considered how the law affects family break-

down, and how it could be changed. Nonetheless, there are many in helping professions who want to "go upstream" to prevent divorce. Such people are immensely valuable, credible leaders and allies.

5. **Grandparents and relatives of divorced families.** They often have more financial resources, time, clarity and objectivity than individuals who are in the midst of divorce or post-divorce warfare. Grandparents want to see their grandchildren but are often prevented from doing so by an ex in-law. They frequently feel their son or daughter, who wanted to save the marriage, was treated unjustly by the "divorce industry."

Cutting Divorce Rates in Half: A 2008 Campaign Issue

What if the Presidential candidates – and those running for Congress, or for state government – were asked, "Would you favor changes in state laws that could cut divorce rates in half, saving 500,000 children from seeing their parents divorce?"

Politicians would probably ask some questions first. Isn't divorce a private issue? How could divorce rates be cut in half? Isn't it the role of state legislatures to write laws on marriage and divorce? How is marriage or divorce a federal issue on which Presidential candidates or those running for the U.S. House or Senate, could have anything useful to say?

Here are brief answers to each question:

1. Isn't divorce a private issue? No Fault Divorce is largely responsible for many of the 43 million divorces since 1970, shattering the lives of 41 million children. While many of them recovered and have built full lives, tens of millions of these children grew up fearful of marriage because they feared divorce. Consequently, they lived together to test their relationships. *Cohabitation soared 15-fold* from 430,000 in 1960 to 6.4 million couples in 2007. As we report in our new book, *Living Together: Myths, Risks & Answers*[55] cohabitation has become the stealth killer of marriage in America. We call it "a double cancer of marriage,"[56] diverting tens of millions from marrying and increasing the odds of divorce of those who do. Few who cohabit understand that one cannot build a relationship based on mistrust.

a) The marriage rate has plunged 50% since 1970. Why? The number of never-married Americans tripled from 21 million in 1970 to 60 million in 2006.

b) Cohabitors increase their odds of divorce by 50%. As Prof. Larry Bumpass of the University of Wisconsin reports, "Marriages that are preceded by living together have 50% higher disruption rates than marriages without premarital cohabitation."[57]

2. How Can Divorce Rates Be Cut in Half? No Fault Divorce should be replaced with Mutual Consent Divorce when couples have children and there are no allegations of major fault, such as adultery or physical abuse. This would change the bias of the law from favoring the destruction of marriage, to one of preserving marriage. The state has an interest in the future of children because studies indicate that they are best reared by their own married mothers and fathers. With four out of five spouses wanting to save their marriage, Mutual Consent would give them a voice and the leverage to save half of the marriages now headed for divorce.

3. Aren't Marriage and Divorce State Issues? Yes, state legislatures write laws on marriage and divorce. However, no state has replaced No Fault with Mutual Consent, though several have considered it. Why? Attorneys head the key committees in State Legislatures. Their bias favors No Fault in part because they feel if one person wants out of the marriage, the marriage is doomed anyway. In addition, divorce lawyers realize huge financial profits.

4. How Can Cutting Divorce Rates Be Made a Federal Issue? As the MADD example illustrates, the Federal Government could give state legislatures a reason to consider Divorce Reform. It might reduce a $10 billion surplus in TANF (welfare) funding by 5% unless the states pass Mutual Consent Divorce Reform.

Background

When Congress passed Welfare Reform in 1996, it pledged to the states that public assistance (then called AFDC, renamed TANF for Temporary Assistance to Needy Families) would continue as a $16.5 billion block grant. One goal of Welfare Reform was "to end the dependence of needy parents on government benefits by promoting job preparation, work and marriage." TANF recipients were told they had to get a job and could receive welfare for a total of only five years. Result: welfare rolls fell by 60%. However the TANF block grant was not reduced to the States, but remained $16.5 billion. Thus, the states have a $10 billion TANF surplus. Thus, it would be reasonable to reduce TANF by 5% if the state were not reforming divorce law.

Two of the most important Welfare Reform goals, as stated in the 1996 law that created Temporary Assistance to Needy Families (TANF) – are directly related to marriage. The first major goal was to "prevent and reduce" out-of-wedlock births. The only way to achieve that goal is for more mothers to marry the fathers of their children. A second goal was to encourage, form and maintain "two-parent families." Again, that is bureaucratic language speaking about the need to create more marriages.

There has been no progress toward either goal – in fact, the opposite. In 1995, the year before Welfare Reform, there were 1.26 million out-of-wedlock births, 32.2% of all births.[58] That number has risen steadily to 1.64 million unwed births in 2006, 38.5% of births. In 1995, 60.9% of all households were led by married couples. That figure plunged to only 49.7% in 2005.[59]

The failure of Welfare Reform to make any progress toward these goals is a second major reason to ask Presidential candidates (and those running for the U.S. Senate or House of Representatives) if they would support a 5% reduction of TANF funds to any state that does not reform its divorce laws.

A U.S. Senator's Proposal for Cutting the Divorce Rate

One U.S. Senator is considering a different strategy that would re-package the $10 billion welfare surplus, to reward those states which reduced their divorce rate, while withholding perhaps 5% of the surplus to fund the incentives. That would give states the free-dom to come up with their own strategy to reduce the divorce rate, such as replacing No Fault with Mutual Consent – or any other strategy. The greater the divorce rate drops, the greater would be the federal reward. The Senator believes the purpose of this pro-posal would be to educate the public about the connection be-tween divorce rates and the health of the American economy.

Document the Cost of Divorce and Non-Marriage

On April 15, 2008, the day Americans pay their taxes, the Insti-tute for American Values held a press conference to announce the cost of divorce and non-marriage to American taxpayers.[60] The report estimated the cost to taxpayers of broken marriages or non-marriages is $112 billion. The report does have state-by-state data which would be very helpful to use in talking to a governor or state legislators. As noted above, Marriage Savers believes the annual cost is closer to $200 billion. Nevertheless, the Institute's report will be an effective resource with state legislators, and will make a persuasive case with state legislators to Reform Divorce. Since even a 1% drop in divorce would save taxpayers $1.1 bil-lion, a 50% drop would save at least $55 billion, according to the Institute. [61]

Mobilize the Churches

The Catholic Church

The Catholic Church, with 65 million members, is so opposed to divorce that the church does not allow divorced parishioners to receive communion, unless they have received a church annulment. Nor will it re-marry divorced people unless they have received an annulment declaring that their original marriage was invalid. While 50,000 annulments are granted annually, that figure compares with about 200,000 Catholic marriages a year. Not surprisingly, *Catholics have the lowest divorce rate of any denomination,* about 25% according to a 2004 Barna Poll, substantially below the 39% divorce rate of Protestants.

Therefore, the Catholic Church, or more precisely, the Catholic bishops in a particular state, might be persuaded to support Mutual Consent and Shared Parenting. However, it will not be an easy task, because Catholics oppose all divorce, and it may be difficult to persuade a bishop to testify in favor of a bill that would permit some divorces. Marriage Savers believes, however, that answer of Mutual Consent would reduce the divorce rate, perhaps cutting it in half in any state that adopted the reform – should be persuasive with Catholic prelates. In fact, Catholic Bishop Gerald Gettelfinger of Evansville, IN, took the lead to create a Community Marriage Policy there in 1998. He has witnessed a 20% drop in the divorce rate and a 16% rise in the marriage rate, serves on the National Board of Advisors of Marriage Savers and wrote an endorsement of this book, agreeing that Mutual Consent could cut divorce rates in half:[62]

"The Catholic Church does not believe in divorce at all, but is encouraged that polls reveal that by a 2-1 margin Americans believe it should 'be harder than it is now for married couples with young children to get a civil divorce (61% to 35%).' How To Cut America's Divorce Rate in Half suggests how to do that, by requiring written mutual consent by both a mother and father before any divorce is granted. By giving the spouse who wants to save the marriage an equal voice with an unhappy mate, many marriages could be restored, perhaps saving most of them," Bishop Gettelfinger wrote.

Evangelicals

A second group of clergy and lay leaders likely to support divorce reform are evangelicals – Southern Baptists and smaller denominations affiliated with the National Association of Evangelicals such as the Assemblies of God and the Nazarenes. Dr. Richard Land, chief public spokesman of Southern Baptists, as Chairman of the Ethics & Religious Liberty Commission said replacing No Fault with Mutual Consent "draws a blueprint for how we can substantially remedy the catastrophe of divorce in our nation, and how ordinary citizens can make a difference." A 2008 Barna Poll reported that deeply committed evangelicals divorce at a relatively low 26%, about the same as the figure for Catholics. In most cities where Marriage Savers has helped the clergy create 200+ Community Marriage Policies, evangelicals have been at the forefront, organizing not only other evangelicals but Catholics, Mainline Protestants and minority clergy.

Richard Cizik, Vice President of the National Association of Evangelicals, wrote his support for this book:

> *"Every pastor is stunned by the number of couples in his church who divorce. Few of them realize that in four out of five cases, one spouse does NOT want the divorce, but is forced to accept it because the law actually grants every divorce, shattering the lives of children. Mike McManus puts his finger on a simple but profound answer: require that in cases involving children, that both parents would have to agree to a divorce, except in cases of adultery or physical abuse. I believe this change in the law could cut the divorce rate in half. That would spare 500,000 children from seeing their parents divorce each year, and save $50-$100 billion in taxpayer funds. This is an issue that should be taken to those running for state or federal offices in this election year."*

Several years ago, NAE wrote an "Evangelical Call to Civic Responsibility" which urged evangelicals to "work to nurture family life and protect children." It notes that marriage is a union only between a man and a woman.[63] Secondly, the NAE identified "easy divorce" as a social evil to be challenged, and committed themselves to foster "good public policies on marriage and divorce law." Certainly 'No Fault Divorce' is such an evil that cries out for reform. It actually encourages divorce, because one partner can file for divorce when the spouse wants to save the marriage.

Mobilize Political Conservatives

Of course, not everyone is religious. However, there are secular conservatives in every city, county and state who are committed to the family. But they have never thought about fighting for divorce reform. Why? Perhaps it is because many of them are divorced, and perhaps initiated the divorce. However, it is puzzling that conservatives who profess to believe in marriage have not taken on the divorce reform issue. In a review of a book by Stephen Baskerville, *Taken Into Custody: The War Against Fatherhood, Marriage and the Family,* here is what Todd Aglialoro wrote for an on-line Catholic magazine, *Inside Catholic:*

> *"For whatever reason, social conservatives focus considerable political effort on abortion, gay rights, and obscenity, but pay scant attention to divorce. Perhaps they think that ship has sailed for good, whereas other battles still offer winnable stakes. Perhaps too few look at our 'family courts' and see a culture war; or perhaps too many lack the conviction to fight it. And when conservatives do target divorce, rather than lobby for legal reform of the 'no-fault' system, or changes in the way courts award custody or child support, they have preferred to employ the tools of ministry, treating divorce primarily as a moral problem rather than a political one; its attendant social evils as a consequence of sin, not of bad policy."*

"This is a grave mistake," says Stephen Baskerville, a professor of government at Patrick Henry College and President of the American Coalition for Fathers and Children. In his path-breaking new book, *Taken Into Custody,* he asserts not only that reforming America's divorce paradigm deserves a far higher priority among conservative culture warriors, but that "Our divorce courts today are agents of radical sexual ideology, occasions of shameless graft, and instruments for the expansion of governmental power at the expense of Constitutional rights."

The Reform Divorce Website

Marriage Savers created the www.ReformDivorce.org website to motivate activists in this battle to reform divorce. We have designed the website to provide the information and rationale to energize these constituencies. We did so in cooperation with John Crouch, of Americans for Divorce Reform, who had already developed his own website, www.DivorceReform.org which includes a wealth of data and studies. We welcome suggestions on how to strengthen our proposed strategy. We also encourage any readers to volunteer as activists who would like to participate in this great cause either locally or in their state or region. Please write to ReformDivorce.org, or call Mike McManus at 301 469-5873.

This book is also designed to educate you and your friends. This book's retail price is $9.95. Marriage Savers will give substantial discounts to those ordering multiple copies: For orders of 10 or more, the cost is $7.95 per book; for 50 copies, $6.95 each; for 100 copies, only $5.95. You can order more copies by going to www.MarriageSavers.org or calling (301) 469-5873.

Reactions?

Here is how Joan D. Ford, who suffered through an unwanted divorce, reacted to our proposal to replace No Fault with Mutual Consent in cases involving children: "Many silent people would love to see the divorce rate slashed. The Presidential candidates could make or break their chance for the Presidency on this issue. The plan for States to decrease divorce by reform or receive a 5% penalty sounds like a winner to me. The stats are shattering that we have let families suffer for so long."

Response from Princeton Professor Robert P. George, McCormick Professor of Jurisprudence

It is impossible to exaggerate the importance of a vibrant marriage culture to the well-being of children and the flourishing of society. The family, built on marriage, is the original and best department of health, education, and welfare. No government program or agency is an adequate substitute. That's why marriage is no mere "private" matter; it is indispensable to the common good.

Yet the institution of marriage is reeling today from many pathologies, including widespread divorce, the social acceptance of non-marital sexual cohabitation, out-of-wedlock child-bearing and child-rearing, and rampant promiscuity. Can anything be done to reverse these trends? Can we rebuild a healthy marriage culture for the sake of our children and grandchildren? Many good people despair, believing that it is too late, things have gone too far in the wrong direction, rebuilding the marriage culture is a lost cause.

Michael McManus begs to differ. He believes—or, rather, he knows, based on work he and his associates have done in communities around the country—that there are things we can do to restore a vibrant marriage culture. Much of the heavy lifting will need to be done by private organizations, especially religious communities, working to restore a sound understanding of marriage and to prepare young people to be true and loyal marriage partners.

But steps also need to be taken in the domain of public policy. For starters, as McManus shows, we need to reform our divorce laws, replacing unilateral (or "no-fault") divorce with mutual consent divorce where children are involved. This reform would, in the words of one prominent divorce attorney, "not only influence the decision to divorce, but the behavior and choices that lead to divorce." McManus recognizes that laws governing marriage and divorce decisively shape people's understanding of the meaning of marriage and affect their behavior and choices. Laws are not neutral. They have an impact—for better or worse—on the marriage culture. Getting the right laws into place is among the most critical tasks we face.

Robert P. George, McCormick Professor of Jurisprudence, Princeton University; Director, James Madison Program in American Ideals and Institutions

ॐ

Chapter 5
Shift Blame From Your Ex To The Law

Decide To Use Your Influence To Help

"Picture this scene. You are an 11-year-old boy. Your Mom and Dad have been drinking and you are awakened by their yelling. As you hear the sound of objects being thrown, you look into the living room. You see your Mom and Dad throwing things at each other. A heavy ashtray flies across the room, missing your Mom. I am the 11-year-old child who witnessed the scene," said Pastor Bob Dailey who transformed the pain of his childhood into becoming a pastor and used these words to explain why he assumed responsibility to create a Community Marriage Policy in Bedford, Indiana in April, 2008.[64]

Are You a Victim of Divorce?

Are you an adult child of divorce with a similar story of pain? Are you mature enough to forgive your parents? This has to be Step One. (In the case of Rev. Dailey, his father's drinking grew into full-fledged alcoholism after his divorce and he died in an alcoholic stupor when Bob was only 20, but not before Bob told his dad that he was forgiven for destroying his home.)

Just as Pastor Dailey turned his misery as a child into a marriage-saving ministry, you can become a leader in a movement to reform divorce. If you suffered from the divorce of your parents, did you realize that this experience may explain why you may have had difficulty building a lifelong marriage? By shifting your focus from your parents or your ex, whom you can't change, to something you can influence, the need to change No Fault Divorce, you will be serving the Lord in an important new cause.[65]

Stop Blaming Your Ex – Blame the No Fault System

Perhaps you are a person who had to accept a divorce you did not want. One such victim told me, "My ex ruined my life. I've lost 24 years of marriage to the woman I loved. I came home from work one day and she had flown across America with one of our children leaving behind our daughter who did not want to be yanked out of high school as a senior. But my daughter blamed me for the divorce. After graduation, she fled to her mother. I rarely saw my own children. It hurt them profoundly. My son did become a physician, but now realizes what his mother did was wrong and now has no contact with her, though my daughter sees us both. She is quite skilled professionally, but has been unable to build a relationship with a man." This anger directed at his wife is understandable. However, the law bears substantial culpability. No Fault always guarantees divorce. If she had been required to get his consent to the divorce, they would have at least had an opportunity to work out their differences.

My hope is that at least some of those forced into an unwanted divorce will decide to shift their anger away from their ex toward the system, the No Fault law that is the evil which is responsible for separating many of the million American couples who divorce each year. One woman who has made this transition of thinking is Patty Fridley. She wrote to ReformDivorce.org saying, "The way the laws are today, it is easier to get a divorce, as a result of No Fault Divorce than it is to break a lease on an apartment. What's wrong with this picture? Lawmakers must realize that laws must be fair. This should include No Fault Divorce which totally disregards the spouse that does not want the divorce. The spouse that does not want the divorce has no say, no voice in the matter. Is that justice?

"No Fault is a great injustice. Laws are created to bring justice to a situation. The law affects the innocent in a devastating way without being able to even speak their case. I might add that it also affects the party filing for No Fault Divorce…There is no equality in this law. The judgment is made before a person even goes into the courtroom. It is a violation to the spouse's rights that does not want the divorce," Ms. Fridley wrote.

"If you think about this law, it does not even make sense. A major problem is that America has such a drive to accommodate self – immediate fixes. That is one reason we got in the predicament of No Fault Divorce. The consequences of No Fault Divorce need to be communicated…Give people a chance to be heard. Even personal stories of how devastating No Fault is and how it has affected individuals' lives.

"The value of marriage, commitment and covenant must be 're-taught' especially in the church. The law of No Fault Divorce should be abolished – totally. This would cover whether there are children or no children and the length of the marriage should not be a factor. Whether you have been married one year or 50 years, there should not be even the option of No Fault Divorce. Once you are married, you are married…Until the law is abolished, there should be adjustments made to the law. There should be mandatory counseling, extended waiting period before finality, opportunity for the spouse not wanting the divorce to have a chance to speak, proof of severity of the situation by the spouse seeking divorce. Why do they want the divorce…There are obstacles to overcome – hardened hearts and a hardened culture. People making the laws do not understand the seriousness and consequences of divorce.

"It is past time. This law must be revisited. Mutual Consent to replace No Fault is a good start. Much prayer…Much action. Luke 18: 1-8. It's time to blow the trumpet. Sound the alarm," Patty Fridley concluded.

Mutual Consent – A Limited Reform

I agree with Ms. Fridley that No Fault is unacceptable. But even she recognizes as a practical matter, it will be difficult enough to simply modify the current law. What this book proposes is that No Fault be changed to deny divorces of couples with minor children, unless both parties agree. It would allow No Fault for couples without children, and to couples who have adult children. Utah's version of Mutual Consent did include marriages of more than ten years. But it was not passed, along with other Mutual Consent proposals. As Patty Fridley writes, "Mutual Consent is a good place to start."

However, to become a leader in reforming divorce, you must move to a new level of understanding – shifting your anger from your former spouse, seeing the issue from a purely personal point of view – to comprehending why America has one divorce for every two marriages.

Most Divorces Don't Involve Severe Conflict

It is important to know that in 70% of divorces, there was no severe conflict like that between Rev. Dailey's parents.[66] According to researchers Paul Amato and Alan Booth, nearly three-fourths of those who divorce have a marriage that seems as stable and satisfying as marriages which survive! Often, one spouse is stunned to learn that a partner wants a divorce, because he or she is happy in the marriage. However, No Fault Divorce allows one person to file for divorce without citing any particular fault in the marriage. As noted earlier, No Fault Divorce really should be called Unilateral Divorce, because it allows one person to unilaterally divorce the other.

Most Divorces Are Unwanted by One Spouse

I cited research earlier that proves divorce was forced on unwilling spouses in four of five cases.[67] There is typically no violence, no adultery, no alcoholism, no abandonment – traditional, accepted grounds for divorce. The law actually encourages divorce because it allows divorce for insubstantial reasons. Often the spouse wanting a divorce explains, "We drifted apart."

Conversely, the spouse trying to save a marriage will often offer to "do anything" to prevent a divorce – see a counselor or attend a marriage enrichment event such as a Family Life Weekend or a Marriage Encounter.

In fact, two million couples have attended a Marriage Encounter weekend where four of five couples actually fall back in love.[68] *In one major study of 4,000 couples who attended Marriage Encounter, 45% of attending couples said their marriages were only "average" or "unhappy," before the weekend retreat! Yet, nine out of ten attendees gave Marriage Encounter high marks for reviving their marriage.*[69] *This is evidence that couples who drift apart can have their marriages revived.*

Divorce Is Always Granted –
Profoundly Harming Children

The law always allows the divorce to be granted even if only one partner wants out. What was entered into by two willing people – can be terminated by one person even if no major fault is alleged, such as adultery, abandonment or physical abuse. A divorce of a couple without children is unfortunate, but it's a calamity if the couple has offspring. They are the innocent victims of the short sightedness of one parent who forced the termination of the marriage. Research is unanimous on the harm of divorce to children. For example, here are three conclusions from *Why Marriage Matters: Twenty-One Conclusions from the Social Sciences,* written by the Institute for American Values in New York, NY[70]:

1. **Mental Illness:** "Divorce typically causes children considerable emotional distress and increases the risk of serious mental illness.[71] These mental health risks do not dissipate soon after the divorce. Instead, children of divorce remain at higher risk for depression and other mental illness, in

part because of reduced education attainment, increased
risk of divorce, marital problems, and economic hard-
ship."[72]

2. **Suicide:** The report notes that suicide rates are twice as
high for divorced men and women as for their married
counterparts.[73] "In the last half century, suicide rates
among teens and young adults have tripled.. The single
'most important explanatory variable,' according to one
new study, 'is the increased share of youths living in
homes with a divorced parent."[74]

3. **Crime:** Even after controlling for such matters as race,
mother's education and neighborhood quality, "boys
raised in single-parent homes are about twice as likely
(and boys raised in stepfamilies are three times as likely)
to have committed a crime that leads to incarceration,"
reports *Why Marriage Matters.*[75]

The Public Supports Reforms of Divorce

A TIME/CNN Poll reports that by nearly 2-1 (61% to 35%), the
public believes that it should "be harder than it is now for married couples with young children to get a divorce." Thus, you can
be confident that the public will be likely to support your efforts
to Reform Divorce.

The Reform: Replace No Fault
with Mutual Consent

As noted earlier, the essential way to Reform Divorce is for states
to replace No Fault Divorce, which is an experiment that has
proven its failure over the last four decades. If there are no allegations of major fault – such as conviction of a felony, adultery or
abandonment – and if the couple has children, a divorce should
be granted only if both spouses are in agreement. That would reduce the divorce rate by 30% to 50% according to experts.

A Related Reform:
Replace Sole Custody with Shared Parenting

On March 30, 2008 a Maryland father was charged with murdering his three children. That reminded David L. Levy, J.D., CEO of the Children's Rights Council, of a similar case in which another Maryland father killed his three children, his ex-wife and himself Thanksgiving, 2007. He acknowledges that mental illness may have been involved in both cases, but adds that both tragedies were "tied to bitter custody battles. These were sole-custody battles in which each parent was fighting to be the dominant primary force in the lives of their children after divorce."

What if the law required that both parents have at least one-third of the time with their children? I believe that in both cases, those children and their parents would be alive and happy. Of course these are extreme cases. However, it is the denial of a parent's fair access to his/her children that has prompted thousands of parents to abduct their children and flee. That, of course, deprives the person granted Sole Custody – of any custody.

Typically, a father gets to see his kids only every other weekend, and is thus virtually excluded from their lives. It is so discouraging to many fathers that they give up. Millions of dads have stopped seeing their children, marry someone else, and forfeit their right to be a dad because it is so extraordinarily frustrating be with their children only two or three days a month. Fortunately, there is a better answer called Joint Custody or Shared Parenting.

What Is Shared Parenting? Some weeks the division might be the children living with the mother during the week and from Friday night through Sunday afternoon with the father. Once a month the situation might be reversed so that the father would have a weekend off. Or the children might remain with a mother for a whole month if they are to be with the father for his two-week vacation. If the children are infants, they might spend a large percentage of time with the mother, but with an increasing percentage of time with the father, as they grow older. Teenagers might live with the father during the week, and with the mother on weekends. The exact nature of the Joint Custody or Shared Parenting would be negotiated by each couple – as long as both parents have at least one-third time with their children. Experts estimate that Shared Parenting would cut divorce rates by another 20%.

Thus, Mutual Consent combined with Shared Parenting could slash your state's divorce rate in half! If Reforming Divorce became a movement across the nation, 500,000 children would not experience their parents divorce each year. That is a goal worthy of your best efforts.

ॐ

Chapter 6
What Can You Do To Reform Divorce?
Eight Steps

1. Meet Your State Legislators

The odds are that your State Representative in the Legislature and your State Senator have never spoken with a constituent who asked for replacing No Fault Divorce with Mutual Consent for couples with minor children, a step that could reduce your state's divorce rate by 50%. See the Appendix (p. 93) for a table that provides data showing how many divorces occurred for the years 2005, 2006 and 2007 for most states. Some states such as California, Indiana, and Louisiana do not tally their numbers of divorces for reasons that are baffling. Why not propose that your Representative or Senator lead the battle to cut your state's divorce rate in half, saving 50% of the marriages a year in your state? There is no better time to do so than in this election season.

2. Create a Citizens For Divorce Reform Committee

Ask your friends who have also suffered as a child of divorce or from an unwanted divorce of their own, to join you in this battle. If each friend recruits ten additional citizens to form a **Citizens For Divorce Reform Committee,** you could talk to 10 Representatives and 10 Senators. Create a Blog, and ask your ten friends to do the same. If each reaches out to ten new victims of divorce, you now have a **Citizens For Divorce Reform Committee of 100** who could become a real political force. One place to start is with a state Family Policy Council, affiliated with Focus on the Family, which can be found in about 35 states. Their mission is to lobby the State Legislatures on family issues. They would likely welcome a citizens' group interested in fighting to repeal No Fault. It might provide professional management of your effort. For a list of Family Policy Councils and contact information go to www.FOTF.org, or call the Family Research Council for an address (202-393-2100).

3. Hold a Press Conference

You could get press coverage if you held a press conference in your state capital, with your Citizens For Divorce Reform Committee, in front of the dome of the State Capitol. You could ask the appropriate committees of the Legislature to hold hearings on the need to Reform Divorce. Give any state Representative or Senator who is willing to take the lead in fighting for reform, the visibility of speaking at your press conference. You could use data published in the new study, released on April 15, 2008, on the costs of family fragmentation, for your own state, *The Taxpayer Costs of Divorce and Unwed Childbearing.* That would suggest how much taxpayer money could be saved in your state if divorce rates plunged in half. The home page of ReformDivorce.org contains a link to the study. Or for a copy, call the Institute for American Values, 212 246-3942, which will tell you to download the study, with state-by-state data.

4. Draft legislation

Legislative drafting is complicated. You may need help from experienced experts. Your state Family Policy Council can provide that expertise. You can also contact John Crouch of Americans for Divorce Reform, (crouch@patriot.net) or me at Marriage Savers for drafting suggestions and advice.

However, below is how Virginia's bill would replace No Fault with Mutual Consent. Others for Utah, Michigan, and New Mexico can be seen at the opening of Chapter 2. Each is a relatively simple addition to current law. It should be added that none have become law. You can see other samples of reform legislation at www.divorcereform.org

The Virginia bill says No Fault "shall not apply if

(1) there are minor children born of the parties born of either party and adopted by the other, or adopted by both parties, and (2) either party files a written objection to the granting of a divorce…"

5. Ask Your Governor to Lead Divorce Reform

No one is more visible and influential than a governor in a state. His/her support would guarantee that Divorce Reform would be debated and considered seriously. If you have a gubernatorial race in 2008, there is no better time than in these weeks before an election to speak to your governor, or his/her opponent.

6. Create a Website Linked to www.ReformDivorce.org.

Each group of activists needs to have its own website that makes a case for reform, and keeps track of how the issue is faring. This website will offer to exchange weblinks with any group organizing in any state. Thus, your work will inspire other states to follow your example. For example, if you are in Alabama, you might consider creating a website, www.ReformDivorce.AL.org.

7. Build a Movement

It is unrealistic to believe that the "ignorance and fear" mentality which dominates current thinking on Divorce Reform by state legislators[76] can be overcome – unless active citizens create a major grassroots movement. That is why we are creating **Citizens For Divorce Reform,** which can have local or state chapters, run by local activists. Here are several suggestions on how to create a **Citizens For Divorce Reform** movement:

a) Recruitment: There are 30 million adult children of divorce and the 75 million men and women who are under court orders due to a divorce. They are the most likely sources of volunteers. Clergy, social workers, and other leaders of the "helping professions" who understand the impact of divorce, can also be recruited as well as grandparents who have lost access to their grandchildren after a divorce. One initial step might be to urge your friends to buy this book. If they are responsive, they are likely to become founding members of your **Citizens For Divorce Reform.**

b) Newspaper Editorial Endorsement: Reforming Divorce is a new issue for the press. As a newspaper columnist for decades, my advice to reforming divorce activists is that you should meet with political reporters to explain why this is an important issue to society. You could also ask to meet with the editorial boards of local newspapers to urge them to support the cause. Chances are, they will ask you as an activist to write a 700-word column making a case for such a step. Better yet, go into the paper with your column asking that it be published. If it is published or the newspaper writes an editorial in support, please send it to our www.ReformDivorce.org website, and it will be posted to encourage others to follow your initiative. (I have posted a sample column you can adapt.) Jesus said, "You are the light of the world. A city on a hill cannot be hidden" (Matt 5:14). Think of yourself as a leader not only in your state, but an example to others.

c) Candidates in an Election Year. Since 2008 is an election year, it is the best possible time to ask your State Representative and Senator if he/she would support steps to cut America's divorce rate in half. If your legislators are uninterested in the issue, go to his/her opponent in this year's elections. If you get an endorsement from either the incumbent or the challenger, help them to organize a press conference to gain public attention for their stand. Make this an issue that candidates will take a stand upon. Two key issues are:

(1) Should couples with children be required to obtain written mutual consent for the dissolution of their marriage if there are no allegations of major fault such as adultery or physical abuse?

(2) Should the Federal Government reduce a state's share of the $10 billion welfare surplus by 5% if a state does not give both parents a voice on divorce?

If you can persuade Obama or McCain to respond, please let me know, so Marriage Savers can give your initiative national visibility. Similarly, if you are able to persuade those running for Congress or the U.S. Senate to support the proposed Federal legislation to press State Legislatures to change the law, by reducing a state's share of the $10 billion welfare surplus by 5% if the State Legislature does not pass Mutual Consent – please call me (301 469-5873). The same applied to candidates running for Governor or the State Legislature or State Senate, if they favor Mutual Consent replacing No Fault.

8. Set a Goal: Enact Reforms in 2009

Marriage Savers suggests that **Citizens For Divorce Reform** Committees set a goal of passing a law to enact Divorce Reforms in 2009. That means you must spark the movement for action during 2008 ideally before the election.

Final Observations

Divorce can no longer be defined simply as a personal issue – a private problem exclusively between two people. Divorce has a wide ripple effect, impacting the couple's children, their children's children, grandparents and future generations – indeed, the general health of our society. Divorce is no longer a problem that the church, the traditional overseer of marriage and counselors alone, can alone try to remedy, however well-meaning. New solutions must be found in government where No Fault Divorce has generated America's excessive number of divorces.

It is time to change the law in order to protect and provide for the future well-being of the family and the institution of marriage. At present the law actually makes possible quickie divorces without considering the dire consequences that impact children. It rewards those spouses who want to destroy marriage. It must be more just. The law should be designed to support those spouses who want to make marriage work for themselves and their children – not empower spouses who want to terminate their marriage often for frivolous reasons, and unwittingly put their children at risk by creating single parent families. Mutual Consent would change those dynamics. It would give an equal voice to the parent who does not want a divorce, and who has not been heared in America since No Fault Divorce swept America in the early 1970s.

Divorce can no longer be viewed as a private matter. It is far more than a personal problem. It is a profound moral and cultural issue. To truly staunch the hemorrhaging of families, we must look to state government and press for reforms that will give a new future to the health of the institution of marriage, the foundation of American society.

One Activist's Perspective

Billy Miller of Alexandria, LA came home about 15 years ago to find that his wife had left him. She filed for divorce and later married another man. That marriage failed. She married a third time, which also ended in divorce. After each divorce, out of his consuming love Billy helped repair her apartment and performed many tasks to assist her. They have remained friends, and he prays she may return to him one day. Indeed, he eagerly awaits reconciliation in their marriage. She is now showing more interest in him, in response to his demonstrable love for her.

Meanwhile, he has become an activist on marriage issues. He writes frequently on marriage, divorce and cohabitation issues to his local newspaper, *The Town Talk*. In 1997 he was a passionate advocate of America's first significant reform of No Fault Divorce called "Covenant Marriage," writing both legislators and newspapers. The bill, proposed by then Rep. Tony Perkins,[77] ultimately became law, creating Covenant Marriage, in which a couple could choose a marriage certificate in which they agreed that it was a marriage for life. If their marriage ever got in trouble, they waived their right to No Fault Divorce and pledged to seek help to restore their marriage and to live apart for 18 months instead of the usual six months allowing time for possible reconciliation.

The Louisiana legislation became a model for similar initiatives in Arkansas and Arizona. In Arkansas the legislation was led by Mike Huckabee, then the state's governor. He describes the initiative in his Foreword to this book: "The soon-to-be-husband and wife agree to structured pre-marital counseling as well as mutually deciding there will be significantly fewer grounds for divorce. Essentially it is a prenuptial agreement, where instead of the traditional form that people sign onto with anticipation their marriage will not succeed, the covenant marriage is where people sign into it with hopes of doing everything they can to preserve their marriage. They not only want to take the necessary steps before they commit, but make sure they exercise all possible avenues before even considering a divorce."

Billy also fought for a second No Fault reform to lengthen the period a couple must live apart before a divorce can be granted from six months to a year. Billy wrote dozens of letters to legislators arguing for the law which he fervently believed would lower the divorce rate because it provided increased time for couples to reconcile.[78] Unfortunately, Louisiana is one of the states that does not add up the number of divorces each year, which means it is impossible to measure any progress as a result of these two bills being passed.

When I told Billy about this book, he wrote me: "You have touched on the concerns of all individuals and organizations that are battling for divorce reform which affects marriages and families. Part of the problem in our battle for reform is that so many citizens are living in the fallout of divorce, that reform does not grab their attention. Stabilizing themselves emotionally and psychologically consumes so much of their energy that they really do not have time to consider other matters."

"We are a 'Gideon's army' or a 'David and his slingshot' against a giant,' but we must NEVER give up."

Remember the Words of Malachi

Malachi, the writer of the last book of the Old Testament has searing words for divorce reform activists:

"You flood the Lord's altar with tears. You weep and wail because he no longer pays attention to your offerings or accepts them with pleasure from your hands. "Why?" It is because the Lord is acting as the witness between you and the wife of your youth, because you have broken faith with her, though she is your partner, the wife of your marriage covenant.

"Has not the Lord made them one? In flesh and spirit they are his. And why one? Because he was seeking godly offspring. So guard yourself in your spirit, and do not break faith with the wife of your youth.

"I hate divorce," says the Lord God of Israel…"So guard yourself in your spirit, and do not break faith." Malachi 2:13-16

Relevance of Malachi to Divorce

Malachi prophesied two major consequences for those who force an unwanted divorce on their spouse:

1. God won't listen to your prayers, because "The Lord is acting as the witness between you and the wife of your youth, because you have broken faith with her, though she is your partner, the wife of your marriage covenant." Unfortunately, the spouse who gets an unwanted divorce also feels their prayers are not being answered by God, even if they have been faithful to the marriage vows. Why? This is partly due to the divorcing partner forcing the divorce. However, I attribute this to the unjust, unconstitutional law called No Fault Divorce. The law forces the divorce every time. Parental anger needs to be directed at the unjust law.

2. God binds the man and woman together as one in marriage "Because he was seeking Godly offspring." If innocent children are forced to experience a divorce that they had no voice in but had to accept, Malachi is predicting that they will become ungodly. Additionally, if there is a remarriage by one or both parents, they will become super-ungodly. It is axiomatic and predictable. Malachi wrote these searing words in 433 BC. They are as relevant today as when they were written nearly 2,400 years ago.

What is the solution? Here is Malachi's answer in the very last words of the Old Testament: "He will turn the hearts of the fathers to their children, and the hearts of the children to their fathers; or else I will come and strike the land with a curse." Malachi 4:6

That quote could be the Biblical motto of **Citizens For Divorce Reform,** the imperative that drives the reform of No Fault Divorce which has separated tens of millions of fathers from their children – against the will of both.

❧

Appendix
Number of Marriages and Divorces by State 2005-2007

About the Appendix

Note several important trends in the Table of Marriages and Divorces by state:

1. The number of marriages fell from 2005 to 2007 in 36 states, even though the population is growing in every state. My home state of Maryland dropped from 38,475 marriages in 2005 to only 35,549 in 2007. Even in Utah, with one of America's highest marriage rates, the numbers fell from 24,109 to 22,640 marriages. This is not a short-term trend. Since 1970, the U.S. marriage rate has plunged 50%.

2. No divorces are reported at all in six states, which should be ashamed of themselves: California, Georgia, Hawaii, Indiana, Louisiana, and Minnesota. How can these states measure any progress if they do not bother to collect the data? The number of divorces rose in 26 states, in contrast to a slight decline in divorce rates in recent years. For example they rose in Missouri from 21,013 in 2005 to 22,377.

3. Most states have one divorce for every two marriages. such as Kansas which in 2007 had 18,564 marriages and 9,157 divorces. This pattern which has existed since 1970 is the basis for saying that America has a 50% divorce rate. However, some people have been divorced two or

three times. Pollster George Barna estimates that 35% of American adults have experienced a divorce.

4. There is a very wide range in the divorce rate between the states. In 2007, Massachusetts had only 14,507 divorces with 38,402 marriages, for a divorce rate of 37.7%. . By contrast, Colorado reports 21,178 divorces and only 29,206 marriages for a divorce rate of 72.5%, roughly double that of Massachusetts. And Mississippi's rate is a stunning 90% with 14,164 divorces compared to only 15,729 marriages.

Table of Marriages and Divorces by State 2005-2007

Each state and Puerto Rico's cumulative figures for 2005–2007 by the National Center for Health Statistics (omitting some states which did not submit divorce data). *By state of occurrence. Divorces include reported annulments.*

State	2007 Marriages	Divorces	2006 Marriages	Divorces	2005 Marriages	Divorces
Alabama	42,382	19,820	42,386	22,867	41,962	22,430
Alaska	5,774	2,953	5,536	2,825	5,446	2,865
Arizona	39,495	24,515	38,983	24,274	38,308	24,535
Arkansas	33,741	16,793	35,088	16,486	35,882	16,728
California	225,832		225,341		228,762	
Colorado	29,206	21,178	33,841	21,139	35,132	20,504
Connecticut	17,328	10,714	19,319	11,027	20,514	10,623
Delaware	4,749	3,858	5,105	3,239	5,015	3,251
District of Columbia	2,143	962	2,297	1,218	2,344	1,145
Florida	157,610	86,367	155,658	85,969	157,976	81,285
Georgia	64,034		66,456		62,893	
Hawaii	27,316		28,679		29,271	
Idaho	15,373	7,372	14,863	7,394	14,935	7,126
Illinois	75,292	32,819	77,981	32,158	74,065	32,408
Indiana	51,219		44,231		43,496	
Iowa	20,061	7,770	20,060	7,949	20,419	8,148
Kansas	18,564	9,157	18,918	8,462	18,804	8,512
Kentucky	33,598	19,677	35,324	21,127	36,251	19,342
Louisiana	32,787				36,569	
Maine	10,095	5,897	10,289	5,608	10,879	5,443
Maryland	35,549	17,374	37,020	17,065	38,475	17,233
Massachusetts	38,402	14,507	37,993	14,621	39,507	14,354
Michigan	59,084	35,450	59,400	35,026	61,108	34,580
Minnesota	29,803		30,952		30,515	
Mississippi	15,729	14,164	16,560	13,955	16,868	12,798
Missouri	39,417	22,377	40,308	22,243	40,675	21,013
Montana	7,126	3,553	7,055	4,192	6,964	4,203
Nebraska	12,417	5,500	12,015	6,095	12,256	5,864
Nevada	126,354	16,593	131,389	16,958	139,572	18,084
New Hampshire	9,364	5,070	9,367	5,322	9,488	5,028
New Jersey	45,435	25,687	47,727	25,794	49,305	25,343
New Mexico3	11,229	8,434	13,423	8,383	12,821	8,837
New York2	130,584	55,943	131,004	59,543	130,409	54,708
North Carolina	68,131	37,412	64,736	35,824	63,384	35,684
North Dakota	4,211	1,527	4,354	1,963	4,388	1,905
Ohio	70,905	37,858	72,783	40,111	74,453	40,181
Oklahoma	26,243	18,750	26,266	19,023	25,755	19,966
Oregon	29,351	14,844	26,679	14,867	26,471	15,033
Pennsylvania	71,094	35,268	71,511	35,330	71,933	29,143
Rhode Island	6,761	2,981	6,990	3,199	7,525	3,159
South Carolina	31,378	14,357	33,852	12,796	35,351	12,423
South Dakota	6,169	2,432	6,303	2,467	6,551	2,159
Tennessee	65,551	29,868	64,505	28,066	65,426	27,823
Texas	179,904	79,469	178,116	79,469	176,768	75,980
Utah	22,640	8,889	23,342	9,904	24,109	9,982
Vermont	5,346	2,364	5,352	2,390	5,525	2,215
Virginia	57,982	29,542	60,235	30,571	62,023	30,052
Washington	41,766	28,925	41,559	26,163	40,802	27,022
West Virginia	12,999	9,026	13,263	9,183	13,418	9,223
Wisconsin	32,234	16,090	33,437	16,730	33,876	16,297
Wyoming	4,847	2,885	4,867	2,690	4,797	2,674
Puerto Rico	21,603	15,454	22,589	17,539	23,523	18,376

End Notes

[1] In fact, Pastor Rick Warren was the subject of a *TIME* Cover Story in the August 18, 2008 issue: "The Purpose Driven Pastor: RICK WARREN: America's Most Powerful Religious Leader Takes on the World.

[2] In 1986, the year Modesto's Community Marriage Policy was signed, there were 1,852 divorces in Stanislaus County, Modesto's metro area and 307,000 people for a divorce rate of 6.03 per 1,000 people. In the first seven months of 2007, there were only 1,709 divorces with a population of 521,000 for a divorce rate of 3.28/1,000. The number of marriages doubled from 1,319 in 1986 to 2,729, much of which is due to that population growth, but the marriage rate rose from 4.3 marriages/1,000 to 4.52 per 1,000.

[3] Mike & Harriet McManus are Co-founders and Co-Chairs of Marriage Savers, 9311 Harrington Dr., Potomac, MD, 20854, and can be reached at 301 469-5873. See .www.MarriageSavers.org. and www.ReformDivorce.org

[4] Paul James Birch, Stan E. Weed, and Joseph Olsen, "Assessing the Impact of Community Marriage Policies® on County Divorce Rates," *Family Relations,* 2004, 53, 495-503.

[5] That number is the basis for the frequent asserting that "There is a 50% divorce rate." However, the figures include those who have had a second or third divorce. Pollster George Barna estimates that 35% of American adults have experienced divorce.

[6] Mike & Harriet McManus, *Living Together: Myths, Risks & Answers,"* 2008, Howard Books, a division of Simon & Schuster, New York, London, Toroto, Sydney, p. 67.

[7] Benjamin Scafidi, *The Taxpayer Costs of Divorce and Unwed Childbearing: First-Ever Estimates for the Nation and All Fifty States,* 2008 Institute for American Values, Institute for Marriage and Public Policy, Georgia Family Council, Families Northwest, New York.

[8] Barbara Dafoe Whitehead & David Popenoe, "The State of Our Unions: The Social Health of Marriage in America 2002," *The National Marriage Project,* Rutgers University, page 2.

[9] In 2006 the Gallup Poll reported that 63 percent of Americans said they are "a member of a church or synagogue," and 40 percent attended services "in the last seven days."

[10] A Gallup study, "Religion in Europe: Trust Not Filling the Pews," reports that "weekly attendance at religious services in below 10 percent in France and Germany, 3-5 percent in Denmark, Finland & Sweden. Data gathered by Heritage Foundation in 2002 based on UN reports, states that when the U.S. divorce rate was 4.1 divorces per 1,000 in a year, it was 2.3 in Canada, .79 in China, 2.4 in Austria, 1.2 in Egypt, 2.0 in France, 2.3 in Germany, 0.6 in Italy, 2.1 in South Korea, 1.1 in Poland. Only Russia and Belarus were temporarily higher after the collapse of the Soviet Union, at 4.3 percent.

[11] Since 1970, there have been 84 million marriages and 42 million divorces, according to data from the National Center for Health Statistics (NCHS), calculated by Mike McManus (See note 13).

[12] Peter D. Hart Research Associates, July, 2003 poll.

[13] Calculations by Michael J. McManus, based on NCHS data. Because several states such as California, Indiana, Louisiana, and in 2007, Texas – stopped publishing numbers of divorces, NCHS no longer gives hard estimates on the number of divorces. Instead, it publishes an estimated di-

vorce rate, which was 3.6 per 1,000 people in 2005. I got the population for each year and made a hard estimate. One wonders why the U.S. stopped making small grants to cover divorce data collection to the states, while continuing to provide funds for unemployment calculations, for example.

14 Mike & Harriet McManus, *Living Together: Myths, Risks & Answers,* Howard Books, a Division of Simon & Schuster, New York, (2008).

15 The National Marriage Project at Rutgers University cites Census data that in 1970 there were 76.5 marriages per 1,000 women. By 2005 that fell to only 38.7 marriages/1000. That is a 50.7% plunge.

16 Larry Bumpass, James Sweet and Andrew Cherlin, "The Role of Cohabitation in Declining Rates of Marriage," *Journal of Marriage and the Family* 53, (November, 1991): 913-27

17 Census Bureau's Robert Bernstein gave the 1970 figure in a phone interview Aug. 6, 2008

18 In this book, I upper case the phrase as No Fault Divorce, though it is often described in lower case, with a hypen, "no-fault." I believe No Fault is such a radical departure from centuries of the law that its nature needs to be emphasized. If quoting other sources with lower case, however, they remain unchanged. I also upper case Mutual Consent, to describe the proposed reform, giving it equal dignity. However, in quoting others, who usually lower case No Fault, I did not change their style.

19 Maggie Gallagher and Prof. Douglas Allen, "Does Divorce Law Affect the Divorce Rate? A Review of Empirical Research 1995-2006."

20 Frank Furstenberg and Andrew Cherlin, *Divided Families* (Cambridge, MA: Harvard University Press, 1991, p. 22.

21. James Sunderland married Bronte Sunderland in 1962, seven years before Reagan signed the first No Fault law. He argued his marriage *was* reconcilable, admitted "deep sorrow" for his failure in the marriage, expressed an "abiding and deep love" for his wife and reaffirmed his commitment to the original vows. He appealed his divorce to the California Supreme Court and then to the U.S. Supreme Court, and quoted Chief Justice John Marshall the 1819 decision, but the state and U.S. Supreme Courts refused to hear the case.

22 "ULC to Meet – for 100th Time," the National Law Journal, July 29, 1991. p. 3

23 Excerpt from a letter to the Commissioners on Sept. 26, 1969 by Hon. Louis H. Burke, Associate Justice of the California State Supreme Court.

24 "The Uniform Divorce Project – the Inside Story of 'no-fault' divorce in the U.S., a report on www.uniformdivorce.com – which is an excellent source for additional background.

25 Ibid. The full text of the Atlantic Monthly article can be found on www/uniformdivorce.com.

26 Judy Parejko, *Stolen Vows: The Illusion of No-Fault Divorce and the Rise of the American Divorce Industry,* 2002, InstantPublisher, Collierville, TN.

27 Hillary R. Clinton, *It Takes a Village, and Other Lessons Children Teach Us,* Simon & Schuster, 1996, pp. 39-40.]

28 Pat Fagan and Robert Rector, "The Effects of Divorce on America," Heritage Foundation Backgrounder.

29 Elizabeth Marquardt, *Between Two Worlds: The Inner Lives of Children of Divorce,* 2005, Crown Publishers, New York.

30 Judith S. Wallerstein, Julia M. Lewis, Sandra Blakeslee, *The Unexpected Legacy of Divorce: A 25 Year Landmark Study,* 2000, Hyperion, New York

31 "The Taxpayer Costs of Divorce and Unwed Childbearing: First-Ever Estimates for the Nation and All Fifty States," a paper by the Institute for American Values, Institute for Marriage and Public Policy, Georgia Family Council, Families Northwest, April 15, 2008.

[32] TIME-CNN Poll on Divorce. For details, see http://patriot.net/~crouch/wash/timetable.html. To see other polls, go to www.DivorceReform.org.

[33] Interview by phone, August 15, 2008.

[34] Linda Waite and Maggie Gallagher, *The Case for Marriage: Why Married People Are Happier, Healthier and Better Off Financially* (New York) Doubleday, 2000, p. 13.

[35] Ibid., page 148.

[36] Larry Bumpass, James Sweet and Andrew Cherlin, "The Role of Cohabitation in Declining Rates of Marriage," *Journal of Marriage and the Family* 53, (November 1991) 913-927.

[37] Frank Furstenburg and Andrew Cherlin, *Divided Families,* (Cambridge, MA, Harvard Univesity Press, 1991, p. 22.

[38] Pat Fagan and Robert Rector, "The Effects of Divorce on America," Heritage Foundation Backgrouder, 2000.

[39] Marriage Savers has worked with 10,000 pastors and priests in 223 cities to create a Community Marriage Policy that drives down divorce and cohabitation rates. For more information on Marriage Savers, see www.marriagesavers.org.

[40] Linda Waite and Maggie Gallagher, *The Case for Marriage: Why Married People Are Happier, Healthier and Better Off Financially* (New York) Doubleday, 2000, p.13.

[41] Paul Amato and Alan Booth, "The Anti-Divorce Revolution," *The Weekly Standard,* December, 1997.

[42] Ibid, p. 131.

[43] With divorce or separation the cause of nearly half of single parents bringing up children, perhaps $50 billion of the $112 billion public cost can be attributed to divorce, vs. non-marriage. If divorce rates were cut in half, perhaps $20 billion might be saved, not $25 billion since some subsidies such as food stamps would remain, but be reduced.

[44] Both *Marriage 911* and the kit to create a Stepfamily Support Group can be ordered from Marriage Savers, 9311 Harrington Drive, Potomac, MD 20854.

[45] For more information on Marriage Savers, see www.marriagesavers.org.

[46] Mike & Harriet McManus, *Living Together: Myths, Risks & Answers,* 2008, Howard Books, a division of Simon & Schuster, New York, London, Toronto, Sidney.

[47] John Witte, Jr. & Eliza Ellison, editors, *Covenant Marriage in Comparative Perspective,* article by Katherine Shaw Spaht, "The Modern American Covenant Marriage Movement: Its Origins and Its Future," p. 262, William B. Eerdmans, Grand Rapids, Michigan/Cambridge, U.K. 2005

[48] *The World Almanac 2008,* "U.S. Population, by Age, Sex and Households," 2005, U.S. Census Bureau.

[49] "Sam Baker" is a pseudonym, but the case is real.

[50] In 1970 there were 196,000 unmarried households with children under age 18 – but 1,954,000 in 2005, according to "Marital Status and Living Arrangements, " U.S. Census, 2005.

[51] *The World Almanac 2008,* "Nonmarital Childbearing in the U.S. 1970-2004, National Center for Health Statistics, which also provided 2006 data in a phone interview.

[52] On July 29, 2008 the Census Bureau estimated that 6.4 million couples were living together at any moment of time in 2007. Over a full year, perhaps 10 million couples cohabited.

[53] George Gallup Jr. cited these polls in a phone conversation with the author on August 15, 2008.

[54] For more information about Marriage Savers, see www.marriagesavers.org.

[55] Mike & Harriet McManus, *Living Together: Myths, Risks & Answers,* 2008, Howard Books, a division of Simon & Schuster, New York, London, Toronto, Sidney.

[56] Ibid, *Living Together,* p. 67.

[57] Larry Bumpass, James Swett, & Andrew Cherlin, "The Role of Cohabitation in Declining Rates of Marriage," *Journal of Marriage and the Family 53* (November 1991 (913-27).

[58] *The World Almanac 2008,* "Nonmarital Childbearing in the U.S. 1970-2004, National Center for Health Statistics, which also provided 2006 data in a phone interview.

[59] *Ibid,* "U.S. Population, by Age, Sex and Households," 2005, U.S. Census Bureau.

[60] Benjamin Scafidi, "The Taxpayer Costs of Divorce and Unwed Childbearing: First Ever Estimates for the Nation and all Fifty States," The Institute for American Values," Institute for Marriage and Public Policy, Georgia Family Council, Families Northwest., 2008.

[61] "The Taxpayer Costs of Divorce and Unwed Childbearing: First-Ever Estimates for the Nation and All Fifty States," a paper by the Institute for American Values, Institute for Marriage and Public Policy, Georgia Family Council, Families Northwest, April 15, 2008.

[62] Call Marriage Savers (301 469-5873) for a copy of a letter he wrote in 2006, praising the Community Marriage Policy for achieving these results.

[63] By contrast, many liberal denominations, such as The Episcopal Church, favor gay marriage and are not only losing church members and churches but whole dioceses who are leaving to join conservative Anglican denominations, such as the Pittsburgh and Fort Worth Dioceses.

[64] The clergy of Bedford, IN organized America's 222nd Community Marriage Policy with the help of Marriage Savers, the organization co-chaired by Mike & Harriet McManus, which is the parent organization of this Reform Divorce Initiative. For more information, call Mike McManus 301 469-5873.

[65] Mike & Harriet McManus, *Living Together: Myths, Risks & Answers,* Howard Books, a division of Simon & Schuster, New York, London, Toronto, Sydney, 2008. A signed copy can be ordered for $20 by calling 301 469-5873.

[66] Paul Amato and Alan Booth, "The Anti-Divorce Revolution," *The Weekly Standard,* December, 1997.

[67] Frank Furstenberg and Andrew Cherlin, *Divided Families* (Cambridge, MA:Harvard University Press, 1991), p. 22.

[68] George McIlrath, "Assessing Marriage Encounter," Chapter 3 of a Doctor of Ministry thesis based on 30 academic studies, which came to a consensus that "Marriage Encounter programs have often received affirmations of 80% to 90% in post-weekend surveys."

[69] "Worldwide Marriage Encounter: National Survey and Assessment," a 1990 study by the National Institute for the Family, Washington DC.

[70] *Why Marriage Matters: Twenty-One Conclusions from the Social Sciences,* Institute for American Values, Center of the American Experiment, Coalition for Marriage, Family and Couples Education, 2002. New York.

[71] *Why Marriage Matters: Twenty-One Conclusions from the Social Sciences,* Institute for American Values, 2002, summarizes research such as that by E. Mavis Hetherington and John Kelly, 2002 *For Better Or For Worse: Divorce Reconsidered* (New York, W.W. Norton, et al.

[72] Catherine E. Ross and John Mirowsky, 1999, "Parental Divorce, Life-Course Distruption, and Adult Depression," *Journal of Marriage and the Family* 63 (1) 197 ff.

[73] Gregory R. Johnson , et al., 2000, "Suicide Among Adolescents and Young Adults: A Cross-National Compariosn of 34 Countries," *Suicide and Life-Threatening Behavior* 30 (1): 74-82.

[74] David M. Cutler et al., 2000. "Explaining the Rise in Youth Suicide," *Working Paper 7713* (Cambridge, MA: National Bureau of Economic Research) (May).

[75] Cynthia Harper and Sara McLanahan, 1998, "Father Absence and Youth Incarceration."

[76] See the comments by Chris Freund, V.P. of Virginia's Family Foundation, quoted in Chapter 2: "Major Obstacles to Reforming Divorce."

[77] Tony Perkins is now President of the Family Research Council, which lobbies Congress on behalf of traditional family values, and wrote an endorsement of this book found in its opening pages.

[78] I also provided evidence to legislators who proposed lengthening the time of separation, that it would lower divorce rates. My home state of Maryland requires a year's separation if the divorce is uncontested by either party, or two years if contested. Maryland's divorce rate is the nation's lowest of any predominantly Protestant culture.